Editor-in-Chief and Founder:
    Lyndon H. LaRouche, Jr.
Editorial Board: *Lyndon H. LaRouche, Jr. , Helga
    Zepp-LaRouche, Robert Ingraham, Tony
    Papert, Gerald Rose, Dennis Small, Jeffrey
    Steinberg, William Wertz*
Co-Editors: *Robert Ingraham, Tony Papert*
Managing Editor: *Nancy Spannaus*
Technology: *Marsha Freeman*
Books: *Katherine Notley*
Ebooks: *Richard Burden*
Graphics: *Alan Yue*
Photos: *Stuart Lewis*
Circulation Manager: *Stanley Ezrol*

INTELLIGENCE DIRECTORS
Counterintelligence: *Jeffrey Steinberg, Michele
    Steinberg*
Economics: *John Hoefle, Marcia Merry Baker,
    Paul Gallagher*
History: *Anton Chaitkin*
Ibero-America: *Dennis Small*
Russia and Eastern Europe: *Rachel Douglas*
United States: *Debra Freeman*

INTERNATIONAL BUREAUS
Bogotá: *Miriam Redondo*
Berlin: *Rainer Apel*
Copenhagen: *Tom Gillesberg*
Houston: *Harley Schlanger*
Lima: *Sara Madueño*
Melbourne: *Robert Barwick*
Mexico City: *Gerardo Castilleja Chávez*
New Delhi: *Ramtanu Maitra*
Paris: *Christine Bierre*
Stockholm: *Ulf Sandmark*
United Nations, N.Y.C.: *Leni Rubinstein*
Washington, D.C.: *William Jones*
Wiesbaden: *Göran Haglund*

ON THE WEB
e-mail: eirns@larouchepub.com
www.larouchepub.com
www.executiveintelligencereview.com
www.larouchepub.com/eiw
Webmaster: *John Sigerson*
Assistant Webmaster: *George Hollis*
Editor, Arabic-language edition: *Hussein Askary*

EIR (ISSN 0273-6314) *is published weekly
(50 issues), by EIR News Service, Inc.,
P.O. Box 17390, Washington, D.C. 20041-0390.
(703) 777-9451*

European Headquarters: E.I.R. GmbH, Postfach
Bahnstrasse 9a, D-65205, Wiesbaden, Germany
Tel: 49-611-73650
Homepage: http://www.eirna.com
e-mail: eirna@eirna.com
Director: Georg Neudecker

Montreal, Canada: 514-461-1557

Denmark: EIR - Danmark, Sankt Knuds Vej 11,
basement left, DK-1903 Frederiksberg, Denmark.
Tel.: +45 35 43 60 40, Fax: +45 35 43 87 57. e-mail:
eirdk@hotmail.com.

Mexico City: EIR, Sor Juana Inés de la Cruz 242-2
Col. Agricultura C.P. 11360
Delegación M. Hidalgo, México D.F.
Tel. (5525) 5318-2301
eirmexico@gmail.com

Canada Post Publication Sales Agreement
#40683579

Postmaster: Send all address changes to *EIR*, P.O.
Box 17390, Washington, D.C. 20041-0390.

Signed articles in *EIR* represent the views of the
authors, and not necessarily those of the Editorial
Board.

Obama Wades Deeper Into the Sea of Blood

Obama Wades Further Into the Sea of Blood

Nov. 29—If you didn't already know that Obama is a serial murderer, and that, for example, he has a "Terror Tuesday" meeting every week in the White House to choose the next round of murder victims from what are called "baseball cards,"—if you're one of the few who has managed to remain ignorant of this for almost seven years,—then a decision handed down on November 23 from the U.S. Court of Appeals for the Second Circuit, will remind you of what the rest of us have long known.

That decision, as reported by Marcy Wheeler and also by Cora Currier, makes it clear that Obama's lawyers are busy cooking up new, secret, "legal" justifications for Presidentially ordered murders, including murders of U.S. citizens. Do you still remember the secret legal opinions written by John Yoo and others in the Bush Administration? Well, Obama is doing exactly the same thing, but he's doing it wholesale.

The Court had been at the point of releasing a 2002 Bush Justice Department memo on Ronald Reagan's Executive Order 12333, which prohibits assassinations by the U.S. government. (It contains some other provisions as well.) The Court's hearing record and its opinion, made it clear that the issue involved Presidential assassinations. For one thing, it cites speeches by Obama's then State Department lawyer Harold Koh, by his then Attorney General Eric Holder, and by Obama's then Assistant to the President John Brennan,—all of them justifying Obama's right to murder at will.

Obama officials intervened to insist that this 2002 Bush Administration memo justifying Presidential murders, remain classified. Why? Only because lawyers acting under Obama's orders, are using that memo right now as raw material to cook up new secret "legal" opinions, "legalizing" Obama's murders.

Another blatant coverup by Obama for his own murders occurred on Nov. 25, when the Army leaked to the press its phony investigative report on Obama's Oct. 3 mass murder at the Doctors without Borders (MSF) hospital in Kunduz, Afghanistan, where 30 or 31 patients and staff were massacred in the space of an hour by a U.S. warplane, while the doctors frantically telephoned the U.S. Army, which already had the coordinates of the hospital.

The phony investigative report blamed low-ranking U.S. service members and supposed equipment malfunctions. But Doctors without Borders does not accept it. That report raises "more questions than answers," said MSF General Director Christopher Stokes. What about MSF's hour-long record of documented telephone calls to the U.S. military to stop the bombing? And why are these damning reports being released the day before Thanksgiving (when the U.S. press is guaranteed to ignore them)?

Obama is plausibly a Satanic personality, said Lyndon LaRouche. He has all the characteristics. Why is he still President? Isn't there something wrong with our constitutional processes? Aren't they being violated? Isn't this treason against the Constitution? But cowardice makes traitors of us all.

Mass killings: Never forget—Columbine, Sandy Hook, Kunduz...

EIR Contents

www.larouchepub.com Volume 42, Number 48, December 4, 2015

Cover This Week

US drone killed 17 innocent civilians in Ra'ada, Yemen in 2013

Obama Wades Deeper Into the Sea of Blood

Obama's Shootdown of Russian Military Plane Puts the World On the Edge of Thermonuclear War

Below is the transcript of the International LaRouche PAC Webcast for Friday, November 27, 2015 .

Megan Beets: Good evening. It's November 27, 2015. My name is Megan Beets, and I'd like to welcome all of you to our regular Friday evening broadcast here at LaRouche PAC. I'm joined in the studio tonight by Jason Ross and I'm also joined, via video, by Jeffrey Steinberg.

Now in discussions earlier this week, Mr. LaRouche made it very, very clear that the key issue facing all of us, is whether the people of the United States, in particular, both the people in positions of leadership, such as the Congress, but also the population in general, have the guts to stop compromising with Obama, to tell the truth, and to throw him out.

Now, what we've seen shaping up over the past weeks is a very dramatically and a very rapidly shifting world strategic situation, including ongoing Russian military intervention into Syria; also including the recent wave of terrorist attacks, such as the bombing of the Russian plane over Egypt, and of course, the terrorist attacks which occurred just two weeks ago in Paris, which were followed by a shift in dynamic among world leaders, away from the failed Obama policy, and toward broader collaboration with the Russians to defeat ISIS.

However, throughout all of this, Mr. LaRouche has been unequivocal that unless, and until, you get Obama out of the U.S. presidency, the world stands on a razor's edge of thermonuclear war.

Now the spectre of that danger arose sharply this Tuesday, with the Turkish shooting down of a Russian plane which was involved in operations near the Turkish-Syria border. And Mr. LaRouche immediately issued a public statement which said that "Obama has organized an act of war, and thus endangered the United States, as well as all humanity." He said that it "was a deliberate attempt by Obama to force general warfare."

Now this act by Turkey and by Obama, and its aftermath, has catalyzed a very significant change in the world global dynamic, which we're seeing manifest, for example, in Europe, among other places. This shift is also the subject of tonight's institutional question, which makes reference to the ongoing talks in Vienna which are aimed at resolving the situation in Syria. The question reads as follows:

SAC Helen Farrer/RAF Mobile News Team

The Turkish Air Force was flying an American F-16 like this, when it shot down the Russian SU-24 on Nov. 24.

"Mr. LaRouche, please give us your view of how Russia and Turkey can move once again to collaborate to save Syria under the Vienna process?" So now I'm going to turn it over to Jeff to give Mr. LaRouche's response to that question, as well as an elaboration of the general strategic picture.

Obama's Deliberate Provocation

Jeffrey Steinberg: Thank you, Megan.

Well, I think that the starting point must be to tell the truth as we know it about the events of last Tuesday. It was immediately understood by leading political and military circles in the United States, in Europe, and most emphatically in Russia, that the action that was undertaken by the Turkish government in shooting down that Russian SU-24 over the Turkey-Syria border area near the Mediterranean coast, was something that (1) was ordered top down in Turkey from President Recep Tayyip Erdogan, and (2) that Erdogan would never have undertaken such an action if he did not have advance approval from Obama and the British.

So, for the Russians, this represented a major act of war, and I can tell you that within the U.S. governing institutions, there was a deep and profound split reflected immediately in actions that were diametrically opposite. Secretary of State John Kerry and leading circles within the Pentagon, all the way up to the Joint Chiefs of Staff, immediately activated channels with Russia, knowing full well that there was a very real prospect that Russia would retaliate immediately after this unwarranted military provocation. And so, you have one element of the U.S. command that is not under British control, that moved immediately to at least temporarily forestall a situation that was potentially moments away from a general war between NATO and Russia. And as we've been saying, as Mr. LaRouche has been warning since virtually the beginning of the Obama presidency, any such war between NATO and Russia would very rapidly devolve into a thermonuclear war, in which the overwhelming majority of humankind would likely not survive.

So you had actions. There were red phone line communications activated immediately between those elements in the U.S. Command that were not on the British line, and top Russian officials. The first objective was simply to secure a commitment that the situation would not immediately go to a hot war. In other words, this was the most dangerous situation since, and probably more so, than even the Cuban Missile crisis. Because in the Cuban missile crisis, there was no shootdown of an American or Soviet ship or plane.

On the other hand, President Obama, who was closer to Turkish President Erdogan than virtually any foreign leader, perhaps with the sole exception of David Cameron in Britain, immediately got on the phone with Erdogan and then issued public statements certifying that, in his mind, Turkey acted perfectly within its sovereign rights to shoot down a plane flying over its territory.

Now, never mind the fact that there are serious questions and disputes of whether that plane, that Russian plane, actually ever even entered Turkish airspace. The fact is that, if it passed through Turkish air space at all, number one, there was never any intent—and nobody in Turkey even claimed there was any intent on the part of the Russians—to carry out any kind of military action or provocation against Turkey. And secondly, even after the first 24 hours following the shootdown, the Turks were even acknowledging that that plane, if it ever in fact crossed into Turkish territory, was there only for a matter of brief seconds, and no longer.

Now that also tells you that to shoot down that plane, was a premeditated, pre-determined decision. There was not enough time for the Turkish air force to consult up the chain of command all the way to President Erdogan, and to then get response orders back, and to fire at the Russian plane—all within a matter of a timeframe that at most has been characterized as 17 seconds. So, again, it was a premeditated act of war; and Erdogan on his own never would have undertaken that. It was done in conjunction with both Obama and the British; and therefore, the responsibility lies there.

Sabotaging Collaboration with Russia

Now, let's again visit what the immediate context was of this incident. It occurred last Tuesday at a point that French President Hollande was in Washington to attempt to organize President Obama to join a trilateral military alliance of France, Russia, and the United States, to wipe out the threat of ISIS and Nusra, and all allied organizations inside Syria and inside Iraq primarily. And so, the events that took place just as Obama and Hollande were sitting down, hijacked the agenda of that discussion.

All you have to do is read the transcript, or even better, watch the video of the press conference that took place later that same day between Obama and Hol-

President Obama grips French President Hollande during their Nov. 25 press conference.

stripes.com

Let's not forget that there was another major series of provocations directed against Russia over the same recent timeframe of the last week. The Right Sector—the neo-Nazi apparatus in Ukraine, that is openly backed and promoted by the Obama administration principally through Victoria Nuland, the Assistant Secretary of State for European and Eurasian Affairs—carried out a bombing campaign against the power grid of Crimea and has effectively shut off almost all power to the entire Crimean peninsula.

When Russian repair units attempted to get to the sites to re-establish the power links, they were fired on by Right Sector militias. To make matters even worse, at the end of last week, it was announced by Nuland's pet prime minister, Arseniy Yatsenyuk, that henceforth all Russian flights over Ukrainian airspace were cancelled. Now, that's tantamount to a threat of yet a second country, a major ally of the United States and the British, threatening to carry out unprovoked strikes against Russian aircraft flying over Ukrainian airspace.

So you've got a clear pattern here. You have—as Megan indicated—a phase shift with the series of ISIS terrorist attacks over the last several weeks, that began with the bombing of the Russian Metrojet flight over the Sinai; followed with a series of suicide bombings on the southern portions of Beirut in Lebanon, targetting the Shi'ite area of that city. And then the Paris attacks. The world was energized to finally launch an all-out serious campaign against the Islamic State. Russia escalated the bombing campaign against the Islamic State and knocked out an estimated 1,000 of the tanker trucks that have been smuggling oil from the ISIS-controlled areas of northern Syria into Turkey, where it has been sold on the black market; and these funds have been fueling the operations of the Islamic State.

At the G-20 summit meeting that ironically took place in Turkey just days before the Turkish air force shot down the Russian SU-24, President Putin made very clear that Russia has aerial photographs showing lengthy caravans of these oil tanker trucks crossing the border into Turkey from northern Syria; and furthermore, he said he has the names of financial agents in 40 countries, including a number of the G-20 member

lande, and you'll see towards the end, Obama launching into a typical Obama tirade against Putin and against Russia. Obama was lying pathologically in saying that the United States is leading a coalition of over 60 countries, and that Russia, when it comes to fighting against the Islamic State, is "the outlier"; and it went on from there. Statements soon after that, again from the White House, fully endorsed and adopted the Turkish line on what happened.

Here you've got a situation where an act of war, an act of military aggression took place, was carried out by Turkey—a NATO member—and was done with the full at least tacit backing of the President of the United States, with the full support of the British. How close do you have to get to provoking thermonuclear war before enough people in Congress and in the American population wake up and recognize that Lyndon LaRouche has been right for years in warning about the menace that President Obama represents if he's allowed to continue to remain in office?

We're down to the final 14 or so months of his Presidency, but you can see the kind of developments that can occur on literally a moment's notice. And so, there is no option any longer other than removing the President from office by Constitutional means immediately. That means that the leading members of Congress, and at least leading elements within the American population, have got to finally wake up to strategic reality.

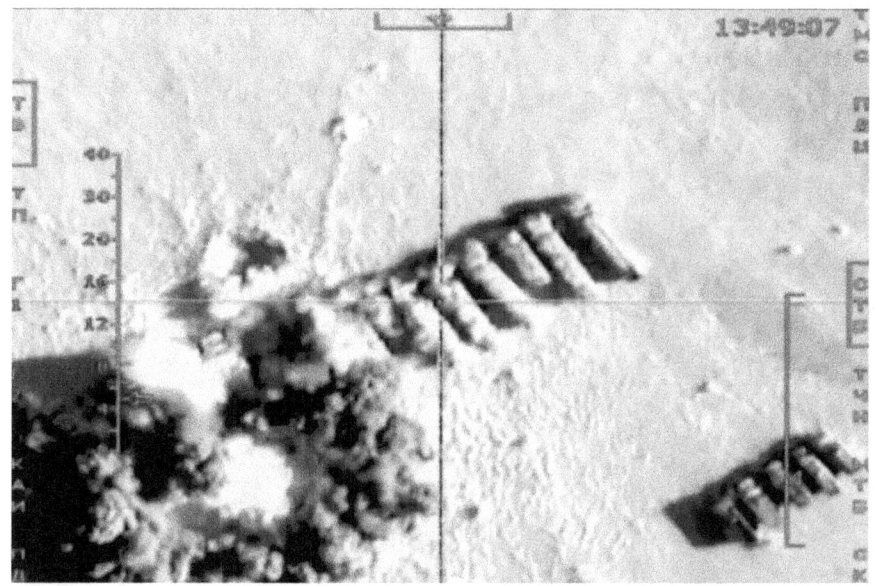

Russian Ministry of Defense

An aerial photograph of the Russian bombing of tanker vehicle columns, which are transporting oil ISIS uses to fund its operations. Published Nov. 18.

countries, that are involved in financing the Islamic State through black market cooperation.

So, the case is unambiguous. If you wanted to attribute narrow motives, you could say that Erdogan was furious at the Russians for bombing these Turkish smuggling trucks, since as we know, the funds generated on the Turkish side from this black market activity largely go into the coffers of the ruling AKP Party. We know that the son of President Erdogan is himself one of the major people involved in this black market operation.

The British/Obama Road to World War III

But that's a much too narrow understanding of what happened here. It eliminates the crucial question, which is that Obama and the British were behind this, and it was an attempt on a much grander scale to not just sabotage the Vienna initiatives, but to trigger a potential world war. And for that crime alone, despite the fact that there is a long list of constitutional violations and other crimes committed by this President, for that reason alone he must be immediately removed from office.

Therefore, every person listening to this broadcast, all of your friends, all of your neighbors, all of your political associates, your co-workers, are going to have to do some serious soul-searching; because we came inches away from world war last Tuesday morning, with the Turkish actions. And it was only a matter of intervention, but particularly restraint on the part of Russian President Putin and the Russian military, that averted it.

There is still clearly an option, and lessons to be learned from this provocation, that could and must lead to reaching an agreement in Vienna to end the five-year war and tragedy in Syria. But that must start with the kind of blunt truth which we have been discussing here over the last few minutes, and it cannot go forward so long as President Obama remains in office.

So, there are urgent issues that must be taken up by the Congress and by the American people, if we are going to avert a war. Because I can assure you, if those critical actions are not taken in the immediate days ahead, then the chances that there will be *another* incident; *another* provocation, whether by Ukraine, whether by Erdogan and the Turks, whether by ISIS, and if actions aren't taken to solve the problem at its roots, we will be staring at the prospect of world war in the immediate days, perhaps hours ahead.

Defeat COP21 Conference of Depopulation

Beets: Thank you very much, Jeff. Coming up this Monday, November 30th, we have the beginning of a two-week long genocidal COP21 depopulation climate conference, which is occurring in Paris, and despite the actual danger to humanity which Jeff just outlined in detail, and especially in the wake of the terrorist attacks in Paris just two weeks ago, this absolutely insane conference is going ahead as scheduled, to be attended by approximately 140 heads of state, along with thousands of other governments, NGOs, and other officials. Notably, Britain's Prince Charles—the dysfunctional and inbred son of Queen Elizabeth and her walking-dead husband, Prince Philip—will be one of the keynote speakers.

Now, as we addressed in this webcast last week, if anyone involved had any morality, we would completely change the nature of the conference, to address the actual dangers and threats to humanity, such as the refugee crisis, the conditions of poverty around the world, and the lack of development, which are actually threatening the lives of billions of people. So I'd like to ask Jason Ross to come to the podium to address this upcoming conference in the context of what Jeff has just presented.

CHOGM

Queen Elizabeth II during the welcoming ceremony at the Malta Commonwealth Heads of Government Meeting Nov. 26.

Jason Ross: This is almost like the worst joke you could imagine, holding this conference in Paris. This conference starting in a few days,—we've been opposing this, and we've got a leaflet, a resolution that we've been getting out on this, called, "We Say NO to the Paris COP21 CO_2 Reduction Scheme." I want to read its opening and closing.

It opens:

The conditions of life for billions of people depend upon rejecting the agenda being presented at the 2015 UN Climate Change Conference to be held in Paris this December. The COP21 Paris initiative to adopt a legally binding agreement to reduce CO_2 emissions must be rejected on two grounds: the scientific reality, that mankind's activity is *not* going to cause catastrophic climate change, and the very real, lethal consequences of the CO_2 reduction programs being demanded.

It ends:

Energy-intensive scientific, technological, and economic growth is essential to human existence. This can be measured by transitions to higher levels of energy flux-density per capita and per area. Such progress, growth, and development is the universal right of man, and CO_2

emissions are presently a vital part of that process for the overwhelming majority of the world's population. The adoption of a legally binding CO_2 reduction scheme at the COP21 conference in Paris will condemn billions of people to a lower quality of life, with higher death rates, greater poverty, and no ability to exercise their inherent human right to participate in the creation of a better future for society as a whole. This is deeply immoral. For these reasons, the CO_2 reduction scheme of the COP21 conference in Paris must be rejected.

So, on the grounds of the fakery of the science, and the very, very real human costs of trying to meet the CO_2 reduction goals, this can't go forward. However, obviously the push is there, the conference is going ahead despite the state of emergency currently in France, the terrorized population of Paris, changes in some of the agenda, but it's going ahead, and as a matter of fact, this conference is getting a kick-start over the weekend—today and the rest of the weekend—the Commonwealth Heads of Government meeting is taking place in Malta. So this is where all the members of the former British Empire, now called the British Commonwealth, get together to—as in this case—hear speeches from the Queen and others about why they need to reduce CO_2.

Dump the Evil Lunatics

Prince Charles—who has been basically waiting for his mother to die for a half century to get a job—said that the terrorism that we're seeing, the conflicts that we're seeing, are not because of the wars, not because of ISIS, not because of the Brits and Saudi Arabia helping ISIS. Instead, Prince Charles said, "In fact, there is very good evidence indeed that one of the major reasons for this horror in Syria was a drought that lasted for about five or six years, which meant that huge numbers of people in the end had to leave the land." This is the guy that they're asking to give the keynote address at the COP21 conference—a man whose understanding of Syria seems to be that all of the conflict is because of a drought which was caused

FIGURE 1
The Proposed 42,000-Mile-Long Network of National Electrified Rail

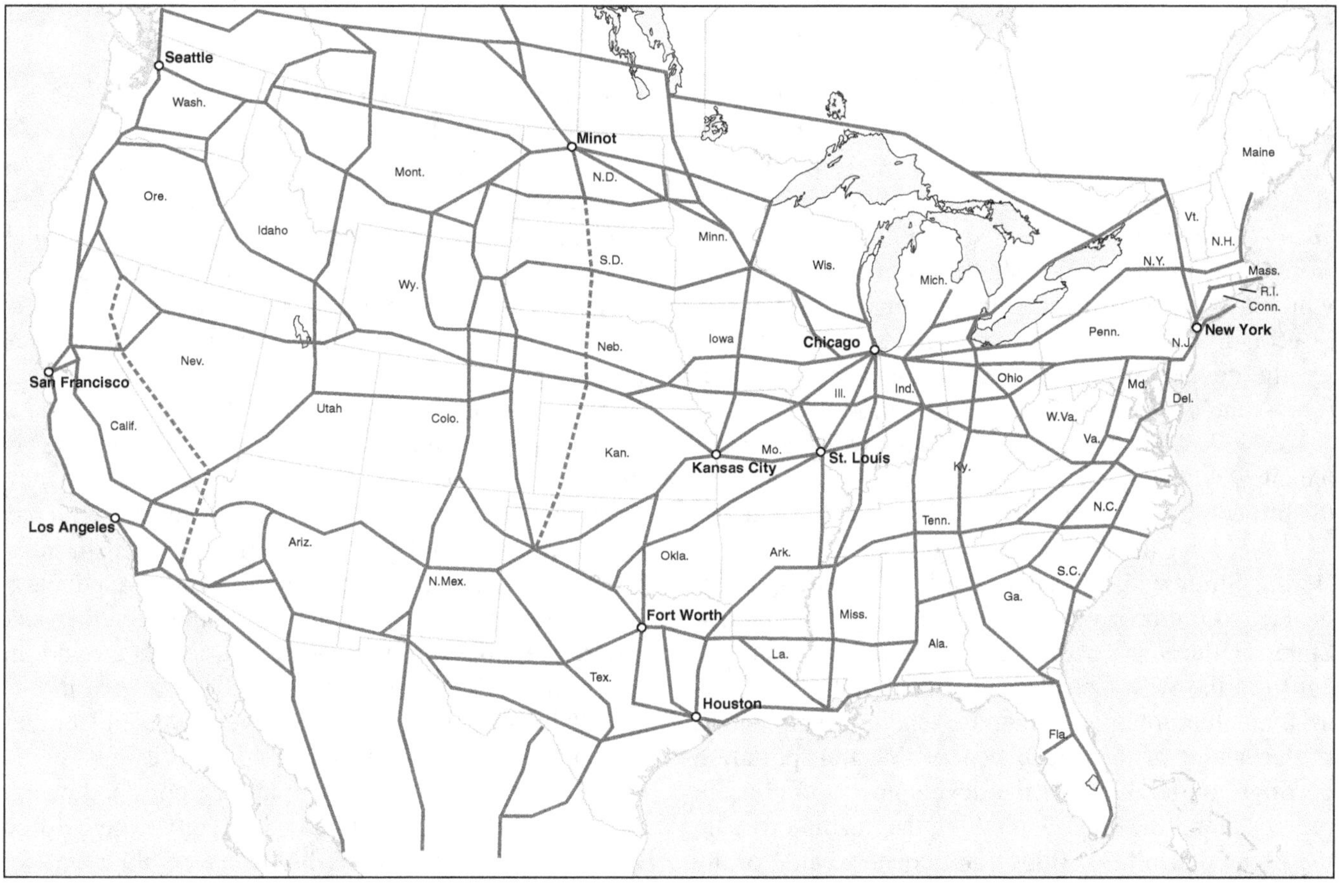

by climate change. It's insane, and it's knowingly evil on his part.

So, what should be done instead, is to re-purpose the conference, recycling what's going to be done there. As Megan said, of course, addressing the refugee crisis, which is all over Europe at present, and beyond—that's worth discussing. Really, what's worth discussing is a solution to this whole problem, which would be excellent.

If the U.S. Congress were to release the 28 pages, put them in the record, as Senator Mike Gravel did with the Pentagon Papers, to be able to attack the cause of this conflict at its source, which as Jeff went through, as LaRouche has been stressing, is Obama, who by his nature as a killer personality, has qualified himself to be inserted into his role as President. That is the cause of the conflicts. Releasing the 28 pages, discussing how to actually shut down terrorism in the region, working *with* Russia on this—Russia is serious about this—that would be worth discussing.

A U.S. Recovery with the New Silk Road

What would it mean to develop the world into the Silk Road? *EIR* released, about a year ago now, *The New Silk Road Becomes the World Landbridge*. It's an almost 400-page report. It goes through in incredible detail, with maps and diagrams, what it would mean for China's One Belt One Road project, its New Silk Road project, to continue its extension into a worldwide paradigm of development.

What would those projects look like? And this is a policy that the LaRouches have been promoting for decades, and Helga LaRouche in her visits to China is acknowledged as "the Silk Road Lady" for her role in bringing this outlook to the current fruition that it's achieving. So what would it mean for the United States to join the Silk Road? What would it mean for us to get our act together?

Well, we've been working on a report on this, in terms of what a U.S. recovery would look like, and there are a lot of aspects to this. If you think about the kinds of projects that have—many—been on the books for decades, and the kinds of projects that will drive us into the future, you recognize that it would not be very difficult to create millions of jobs in a very short period of time—meaningful, productive jobs—that lay the groundwork for a durable and new, more productive economy for the future. Doing that will require getting Glass-Steagall re-implemented—having those provisions back in place, and shutting down Wall Street, which we do not need. Gambling is not an essential part of economy. The productive process, science, creativity, the development of human beings and infrastructure—that is essential. Gambling is not.

So with Wall Street out of the way, with federal financing, with federal credit made available, some of the projects are things that we've discussed quite a bit.

Take, for example, the Bering Strait. Crossing the Bering Strait with a tunnel or a bridge, as engineers decide, would be a very key project, to put the United States on the Silk Road: literally, making it possible to get from the West Coast of the United States into Eurasia, much more quickly than by sending a ship across the ocean, with the added benefit that transportation corridors on land enable the development of adjacent regions along the way. Something that a ship crossing the ocean doesn't do. Ships don't create wealth, or the potential to create it, as they cross the waters. Land connections do.

So the Bering Strait tunnel—that would be a key project. Overall, transportation has a tremendous way to go in the United States. You know, China, which is a nation very similar in size to the United States, currently has 11,000 miles of high-speed rail, with plans to have 30,000 by 2020, and they'll do it—they do what they say. In contrast, we have under 500 miles of high-speed rail, and that's being very generous in counting the Acela service as high-speed. What we should have is 42,000 miles of electrified, decent rail in the United States, bringing down the costs of transportation, and of production, throughout the nation, making it more possible to move intermediate goods from place to place, to move people, to move products in a way that will have a tremendous savings in time, and in energy costs.

Currently over half of rail freight in the United States is coal. In a nuclear economy, we obviously wouldn't need so much coal, but it also goes to show how little else is being done with the system as it is, and maybe some idea of what it could be like in the future.

City-Building Plays Central Role in Development

Along with the development of the basics which we naturally think of—things like transportation, rail, repairing roadways, power plants, water systems, which I'll get into in a moment—the other aspect is cities. Now, India has committed itself to building scores of new cities across the country. Russia has created science cities.

The United States—imagine the potential, not to keep adding more and more sprawl to the outsides of our current cities, but developing legitimately new cities, actual cities, planned in a sensible way, with part of a transportation backbone underlying it, with infrastructure that's needed, such as canals and aqueducts as necessary, water, power, that sort of thing. But then also where the cities and where life is oriented around the most key of economic processes—the creation of wealth by improving the productive powers of labor, by the cultural role that can be played by a city.

In addition to the ability to move goods and people easily—the density you find in a real city, where different members of the household can do their various things that anyone having an hour-and-a-half commute can not—you also have the other role of the city itself as a social institution.

In a very interesting article that LaRouche wrote some decades ago, in a program for the development of Africa, he discusses the central role of the city, and the presence of a research and educational complex, a pedagogical museum where people, kids and their parents, would be able to step themselves through how discoveries had been made in the past in a hands-on way, doing experiments, themselves witnessing and understanding very directly how humanity has gotten where it is, making it possible to have workers able to master new technologies, and scientists able to reflect on what science has done in the past, to create the new discoveries needed in the future.

This sort of educational center of the city will be more than a museum detailing the past; it will be more than looking backwards. LaRouche wrote that to give vitality and direction to the process, the educational zone of a new city must be engaged in some aspect of

> To give vitality and direction to the process, the educational zone of a new city must be engaged in some aspect of scientific research which is itself of world importance.

A depiction of the Great Library of Alexandria, built by citybuilder Alexander the Great, by O. von Corven.

scientific research which is itself of world importance. He said:

> ... a modern nation has achieved true sovereignty in spirit, only if it achieves excellence in some important aspect of advancement of human knowledge generally. A people which can point to several institutions of its own nation, and can identify several important contributions to human knowledge associated with such institutions, is a people which knows that its children are capable of equalling, in importance to humanity, the children of any other nation. To teach science is to teach the principles of discovery.

With cities, with this as an included basis, cities of finite size (no more than one or two million people),

with the development made possible by rail, by water, by developing fusion power on a crash basis, and by implementing the already discovered capabilities for improving nuclear fission power plants, we'll be able to dramatically increase the electrical power available in the nation to power transportation, to power manufacturing. And to do all of this, we're also going to need the revival of the design of machine tools themselves.

The Machine Tool Principle: The Scientific Basis for Progress

Now, machine tools—not everyone's actually seen one of these in person. These are the tools for making machines; they are lathes, drills, milling machines, shapers, and jigs—these are the devices that create metal parts.

To the extent that you are able to innovate in this area, as has been done over the decades using new technologies—such as electric discharge machining around the time of the Apollo program, or electron-beam welding, or more recent developments of laser and plasma cutting, and computer control of machine tools to create things that formerly took ten times longer—to the extent that this technology improves, and to the extent that as part of an industrialization process the capital stock is increasingly of newer, more productive machine tools, the entire economy sees the benefits, because they make all other production easier and reduce the cost.

So, this machine tool principle is, in the small, an image of what it means to take discoveries and then implement them in an economy—for new thought, new engineering, or new scientific ideas, to become manifest in the economy. And this is a field where we need motion. As I said earlier, we need power; fusion research has been starved of funding deliberately for decades, preventing the kind of breakthroughs that would make power too cheap to meter—or even, if not that cheap, remarkably abundant—to bring the next generation of production technologies into play:

• Cheap power to transform our relationship with raw materials, and with the reshaping of those materials.

• Technologies such as the plasma torch.

So, in this kind of economy, we can then re-approach such subjects as water. California is in what's called a water crisis, despite being right next to the Pacific Ocean. Why do we not have the power and the plants in place to be able to desalinate? To at least provide for much of the needs in California? Why have we not done more research on how weather actually functions?

People Are the Only Source of Wealth

One of the ironies of the global warming alarmists, hysterics, whatever you want to call them, is that this supposedly scientific outlook is actually stifling science.

Hypotheses about what's causing climate change over time, hypotheses about how cosmic radiation coming from our Galaxy, or even beyond, plays a role in creating the condensation nuclei to form clouds, to effect precipitation, to change the albedo, the reflectance of the Earth and therefore its temperature—that's real science that's being held back by the global warming mafia, who reject this kind of approach because it doesn't come to the conclusion that they want: namely, that human-made CO_2 is *the* determining factor in global climate.

It's just not true.

As stated in the resolution that I read at the beginning, and as is covered in the *EIR* special report published in September, "Global Warming Scare is Population Reduction, Not Science," the science is clear. We are not causing catastrophic warming of the planet. Mankind is not a virus destroying the Earth. What is destroying the planet is oligarchism, the outlook that human beings are a disease. It is being destroyed by the anti-growth and enforced poverty promoted by the City of London, by Wall Street, by that system, which has to be removed.

In its place, as far as an actual concept of humanity, let me read another quote from LaRouche here. He says, "Every infant born in any part of the world has the potential for development of his or her mental powers to the level sufficient for adult competence in use of modern technology." And this also means real technology, not iPhones. "That child can achieve at least an approximation for practice of the highest levels of productive powers of labor in the world generally today. It

Every infant born in any part of the world has the potential for development of his or her mental powers to the level sufficient for adult competence in use of modern technology.

creative commons/Godot13

Students at the Lukhanyo Primary School in the Western Cape province of South Africa.

is that potential development which is the only source of wealth."

Let's remember that; the source of wealth, the increasing of the productive powers of labor, as Hamilton put it, lies in that ability for human beings creatively to develop new understandings about nature, and thereby re-form the economy in an entirely new way.

That's real economic science, and with that approach—the programs that are needed, the development projects which we can implement, the jobs that they will create—this can all follow from an outlook of what economics truly is, breaking free from the false ideas about it which have been promoted by Wall Street and which have affected, unfortunately, a very great number of our fellow citizens.

Einstein:
The Twentieth Century's Only True Scientist

Beets: Thanks, Jason. Two days ago, on Wednesday of this week, we celebrated the 100th anniversary of Einstein's publication of his paper on general relativity. LaRouche has reiterated many times in the recent period that Einstein was the only true scientist in the

20th Century, someone who held out against the corruption in thinking that was ushered in, in 1900 by Bertrand Russell. Einstein was attacked and isolated for his commitment to the paradigm of thinking which represents the actual human mind; the paradigm which was responsible for all of human progress up to this point.

So I'd like to ask Jason to come back to the podium to address this question: Given the task ahead of us today to rebuild society, rebuild civilization, and create a new paradigm for mankind, can you give us a sense of the importance of Einstein's work and his commitment?

Ross: Sure. I think what Einstein accomplished represents a key concept under which science can be understood, that of metaphor. LaRouche has repeatedly stressed the importance of metaphor as the key to science, meaning the development of language in such a way that you express a new scientific truth in a way that could not even have been stated in the preceding language. It's not something mathematical; it's not a formula or an expression. Discoveries in their true form can't be. After the fact, you might be able to write them down; but what makes them a discovery is an overthrowing of the past, the development of a new basis for thinking that is incompatible with what came before.

That's the kernel of what a discovery is. None of these thoughts are really eternal; what is eternal, is that process of developing new thoughts. That identifies the incredible error in science education today, which is based on understanding how to apply the fruits of discovery to specific problems, but not on going through how they were developed.

One hundred years ago, in 1915, Einstein successfully expanded his special theory of relativity, which he had developed in 1905, into a more general form, making it the general theory of relativity. I want to say a bit about what Einstein did—I think it would be wrong not to—and then get into what it means for us today, what's the relevance. Einstein is not just someone to idolize, or say, "Wow, he was a real genius." Figure out what he actually did.

Going back ten years earlier to 1905—110 years ago—in what's now called the special theory of relativity, Einstein changed the basis on which scientific thought was based. At that time, the prevailing view was the Newtonian outlook on space and time. Isaac Newton had said that space and time were independent

FIGURE 2

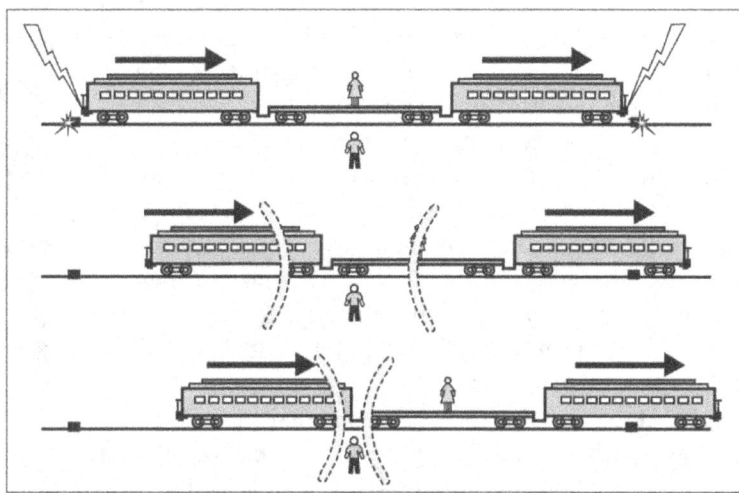

Einstein's thought-experiment on the Relativity of Simultaneity: In the top frame, two lightning bolts strike opposite ends of a moving train. The two strikes are simultaneous relative to the stationary observer standing on the platform, as we see in the bottom frame, where the two flashes arrive simultaneously to that stationary observer. But they are not simultaneous for the moving observer standing on the train's flatcar; in the second frame, the light from the lightning bolt on the right has already reached the moving observer, whereas the light from the left has not. For this moving observer, the lightning bolts were not simultaneous; the bolt at the right occurred first.

of things within them: Space is space; within it, things exist and take place, or occur in different relations to each other. According to Newton, time flows on its own, without reference to the things in it; they take place over time, but time has an independent existence.

Einstein Makes a Revolution in Physics

Well, Einstein tore that apart in 1905, in some ways with rather simple thoughts. For example, he demonstrated that the concept of simultaneity does not exist, that depending on who you ask, and that person's motion with respect to two events that are occurring, that observer might say yes, they occurred at the same time—using the light from those two events reaching him or her, to determine whether one occurred first, or whether they occurred simultaneously. But the *motion* of the observer relative to the two events will affect whether they appear to occur at the same time or not.

He gave the example of someone on a moving train witnessing two lightning bolts, compared to someone on the ground witnessing these events. For the person on the ground, the light from both events happens to reach him at the same time. But the person on a moving train that happens to be at the same point between the two bolts as the observer on the ground, when the two events occur, finds something different: Because of the train's motion relative to the ground, this person is going to see one bolt before the other one.

Who's right? What does it really mean to say "at the same time"? Because all the laws of nature work the same, whether you're standing still supposedly, or you're in constant motion, there's no way to say who's right, what the right time should be. And the idea of having a universality of simultaneity, to say "at this moment in the universe" disappears, and it becomes relative to the observer.

What does that mean? It means that time itself no longer exists as a basis for thought in the way that it had before. There's still time, but it's no longer an untouchable permanence; the same thing is the case for space. Events take place in space-time, rather than in space (without regard for time) or in time (without regard for space). In 1905 in his special theory of relativity, Einstein replaced the concepts of space and time as a basis for physics with something physical—light's motion. In this way, he was implementing one of the revolutions in physics that Riemann said would take place; that our understanding of geometry would take place not by looking at geometry, but by an understanding of those binding forces of nature which give rise to what is then observed. A bent space; a curved space; a skewed space.

With his general theory of relativity in 1915, Einstein went beyond frames of reference which are either at rest with respect to each other or in uniform motion relative to one another; he now considered acceleration. He said that that there is a relativistic equivalence between inertial and gravitational mass.

Let's give an example. Someone is sitting in a room and can feel the floor pushing up against his feet or, to put it another way, he can feel his feet pushing down against the floor. But, unless he leaves the room, he can't tell whether he is just experiencing the gravity of Earth as the building sits at rest on its surface, or whether he is out in space and the top of the building is attached to a rope which is being pulled at an accelerating rate, constantly pulling the building up against his feet. No experiment, nothing you could do inside the room, would be able to distinguish the one from the other. From this equivalence then, Einstein derived his general theory of relativity, by which not only motion, but gravitation changes the shape of space and time.

CC/Damien Deltenre

Experiments done during a total eclipse of the Sun in 1919 helped Einstein demonstrate his theory of general relativity. Here, a picture of such an eclipse taken from Spitsbergen, Norway on March 20, 2015.

This was a very wild, shocking idea, and still is. Space and time were considered to be such fundamental things that the possibility of them even being curved was rejected out of hand by people like Immanuel Kant, Isaac Newton, and Bertrand Russell.

But Einstein was able to demonstrate that he was right. Two quick examples. One was the orbit of Mercury. The orbit of every planet has a place that's farthest from the Sun, and one where it's closest to the Sun. You draw the line through those points on the elliptical orbit. With the passage of time, that line isn't stationary. It actually moves. For Mercury it moves a degree and a half every century. And based on calculations of gravity, as it was understood, people were able to explain almost all of that change. There remained a very, very small—about .01 degree per century—change in Mercury's orbit that no one had explained, but which Einstein was able to explain with his theory.

Also his prediction about how light would bend going around massive objects, was borne out in the experiments during the eclipse of 1919. Photographs were taken of stars near the eclipsed Sun—since the Sun was covered, you could actually see stars near the Sun. The position of the stars (or, more exactly, the apparent position of the stars, based on the light received from them at Earth) was then compared with the apparent position of those same stars when the Sun was not near our line of sight to them. Each star's position was different in the compared images. This showed again that Einstein was right, that the path of light coming from the stars towards us was deformed, was shaped, by the presence of the Sun's gravity.

Einstein Surpassed Old Laws

These are the things that people are most familiar with about Einstein, things that are indisputably advances that he made. But there's more to him than that. I think that the great importance that LaRouche attributes to him—what Megan mentioned—LaRouche calling him the only scientist we had here in the Twentieth Century, the only one who stuck to science—lies elsewhere as well.

The other great work that Einstein accomplished was on the quantum. In 1905, in addition to special relativity, he also wrote a paper to explain the photo-electric effect, and it was actually this for which he was awarded the Nobel Prize later. This expanded the ideas of Planck in showing how light itself must come in particles or quanta, that it's not purely a wave phenomenon, that there's something particle-like about it. Some experiments, however, required light to also have wave-like properties, making it impossible to decide in a simple way on this question. Is light a particle, or is light a wave? This is one of the difficulties of quantum physics.

What Einstein held out against was the interpretation by scientists in his day, led by Bohr, mainly, Neils Bohr the Dane, to say that science had reached a limit; that to ask "why" was really no longer admissible, and that in the quantum world, physics, instead of saying what nature is, is limited to describing how nature appears. Einstein would not accept that. Einstein never accepted the idea that we had reached an end to the ability to know things, and that quantum theory as it was known at that time, was final, complete. Something that's never been true of, really, any theory in history.

This is seen now with the ongoing difficulties around completing quantum theory, and also the anomalies in the fields of life and the potential for a higher understanding of these quantum processes in the field of cognition. It's also seen in Einstein's own work, in the theory of gravitation. with the difficulties—I hope you've been watching the series of presentations our colleague Ben Deniston has been doing on the Galaxy on this website every other Wednesday—it's also seen in the difficulty in understanding the speeds of rotation of galaxies. That problem was the original basis for hypotheses that people make about dark matter now. This may indicate that we have simply reached the limits to the applicability of our physical theories and need to go beyond them.

That's not done mathematically by positing new ways to keep our old laws, to explain the new phenomena, but it can require going beyond them.

So, we don't have answers to these questions. We shouldn't fool ourselves into thinking that we do already have the answers to these questions. And the importance of Einstein for us today, is that of a successful discoverer who overthrew what had been thought, developed a higher theory to explain things, and was guided by an understanding of the role of the human mind in developing new, successful concepts about nature. With that as a basis for how we relate to other human beings, with that as a basis for social relations, we can forge a much higher level of cooperation on this planet, and develop a culture that's really suitable for the human beings who participate in it.

Beets: Thank you very much, Jason. With that, I'm going to bring our broadcast to a close. I would like to thank Jason for joining me, and Jeff for joining us via video, and I'd like to thank all of you for watching tonight. Please stay tuned to larouchepac.com. Good night.

The View From Paris

Nov. 29—Below is the transcript of an interview with Jacques Cheminade.

"This is Tony Papert, co-editor of *EIR*, and I'm on the phone with Jacques Cheminade, former French Presidential candidate and the president of the party Solidarity and Progress *Solidarité & Progrès* in France, and an old, old friend of Lyndon LaRouche."

Papert: Jacques, your President François Hollande was just in the United States, and met with Obama just as the Russian Su-24 bomber was shot down by Turkish fighter jets, bringing the world a big step closer to thermonuclear war. Now, our sources in the government—as do many other people—insist that Turkey's President Erdogan and the Turkish Armed Forces would never have shot that plane down without the prior go-ahead from Obama. And indeed, in that discussion with Hollande, when he addressed this criminal shoot-down, Obama had no words of condemnation for Turkey, but said they had the right to defend their airspace.

You have been following and writing about,—and also very active on the ground politically,—in the French situation over this entire period. How do you view the current developments?

Jacques Cheminade: Well, Hollande—you have to locate him personally and in the situation where France is today. He's not in a position of strength, and he's not himself a strong character. So the French know very well that the main problem at this point is the Turkish border, where all the weapons from Da'esh are coming into the territory of the Is-lamic State, and of course, the oil and the agricultural products are smuggled out, and make the money flow for Da'esh.

What I have said many times, is that if the Western states were truthful, they would shut off all the finances of Da'esh. They're not doing it. They're not intervening in the money-laundering of the Da'esh money by the banks. The only way to stop Da'esh is to cut their money flows, because the Islamic State is not a viable entity. It produces nothing. It's like Nazi Germany. It cannot exist unless it extends its power to other territories, and unless it is allowed to go on with a smuggling strategy.

The French know that very well. But they are in a weak position. If you look at Hollande, first he went to the United States to meet Obama, because what he wants is to get the information from the NGA [the National Geospatial-Intelligence Agency]—he wants that. Obama said, "Why not?" But the CIA and CENTCOM said "no." And when the French asked them why, they said "Obama told us to say no." The double game.

That's one point.

Russian President Vladimir Putin greets French President François Hollande in Moscow Nov. 26.

kremlin.ru

Hollande Turns to Moscow

The other point is that after that, Hollande went to Russia, and he went there not only with [Foreign Minister Laurent] Fabius, but also with [Defense Minister Jean-Yves] Le Drian. It's known that Le Drian and Fabius are opposed within the Hollande government. Le Drian is more favorable towards an entente with the Russians, and Fabius wasn't.

So what happened is, Hollande met Putin, and he said *tu* to Putin [the familiar form of address in French]. He never said *tu* to Obama. That's one thing to be noted. And what Hollande said is that we are willing to work with Russia, and we want to work with Russia. And Putin agreed. But Hollande said, "Don't bomb our friends in the Free Syrian Army"—*l'armée syrienne libre*, as it's called in France. So, Putin said all right, we're doing our best not to bomb them, but let's work together and exchange information.

And Hollande said, yes, we will exchange information, and we'll give you all the information we have. And Putin agreed.

So the people who are against Bashar [al-Assad] were freaked out by that. They said, "Oh, the French are giving information to the Russians; this is terrible. What's going to happen?"

Then, what Fabius said is very interesting. Fabius himself—everybody here is saying Fabius is backtracking—yesterday he looks like a feline, today he looks like a castrated cat. So, Fabius said that well, in the present situation, we have to work with the ground forces of the people who want to fight. So these are the forces that remain of the Free Syrian Army, the Sunni forces against Da'esh, and he added, why not the forces of the Syrian regime of Bashar?—and also the Kurds.

This is entirely new. It goes against everything that Fabius has said before. Because Fabius had praised—I think a year ago—the good work of the al-Nusra Front. But now he's saying, let the Russians bomb it. It's a big change. And Le Drian was standing there just next to Fabius, and this was for the Russians, in particular, a symbol.

The plug has been pulled on Fabius,—the front pages are full of it.

So the cooperation that Hollande said he wanted, international cooperation, has failed because of Obama. So now, Hollande said well, let's pursue coordination and work with the Russians. Now at this point, the information question is key, because the French are relatively blind,—because in France, the internal security, the internal counter-espionage, and the external coun-ter-espionage, the DGSE, are separated. So they need information. They are trying to get information from the Americans, and they are trying to get information from the Russians, and they feel weak because they were blind, or relatively blind, before the terrorist massacre in Paris.

What they are saying now, is we should cooperate. Their eyes, in a certain sense, have been opened, even if it's for opportunistic reasons, but they have been opened.

A French 'Pearl Harbor' Effect?

What's very interesting—and this is not usually mentioned—is the reaction of the French population. They are putting up flags on their walls. Even people who had no flag, are putting up shirts or scarves with the three colors of the French flag. This patriotic reaction is not at all against the Muslims—it's against the terrorists, and people are saying that they can see the difference between these crazy people, financed through what they call here "international organizations," which means Saudi Arabia, Qatar, and others,—they see the difference between these people and the Muslims and Islam. This is a big question now. Even a lot of mosques in France are putting up French flags on their walls.

It's a very interesting situation.

It can go in either direction, because you remember that Chirac had opposed the American intervention in Iraq. And then I told people around Chirac: you should go ahead with Glass-Steagall, and the New Bretton Woods. They didn't do it. So the thing went nowhere.

Now it's the same for Hollande. He has an opportunity to go ahead. If he has the courage to go against Wall Street, and against the French and German megabanks, Deutsche Bank, BNP Paribas, also Societé General—if he goes against them, he will change the situation. At this point, it doesn't look like it, but a lot of people are discussing the issue of national unity. National unity would be a good thing if it's based on principles. At this point it's not clear what it's going to be based on, or whether it's going to happen.

Papert: That's very revealing. And certainly, as you said, these are things which are not discussed in France, but they're things which are not discussed here either.

Cheminade: The French also, I should add, have been shaken by what happened in Greece, because [former Greek finance minister Yanis] Varoufakis told the French that first, these supranational forces are

EIRNS

Jacques Cheminade addresses the General Assembly of his political party in Paris on Nov. 8, 2015.

going to hit Greece, but at the end of the process, it will hit France, and even Germany,—but France first. So the French know very well that if they go along with these interests, they are going to be destroyed by them.

They don't have the courage to go frontally against them, but the population, the French population, is more and more, let's say, conscious of what the French government should do, if it were was a sane government.

The Threat of world War

Papert: I began by noting that the Russian bomber was shot down by the Turks just as Hollande and Obama were about to meet. And as I said, our sources here, particularly in the U.S. military, on the one hand say what I said—that would not have happened without a go-ahead by Obama—and on the other, they're extremely agitated and concerned and active against what they see as a much more imminent threat of all-out war beginning between basically the United States and Russia.

You are close to many high people in the French administration, even if you are somewhat publicly a black sheep. Can you tell us more about that from your point of view?

Cheminade: What they say in private is that there is an imminent threat of World War III, and that with all these planes from various countries flying over Syria, anything can happen. They say it's even more dangerous than Ukraine. And also there is the possibility of a new terrorist attack in France, or in any other country, but particularly in France, because they want to stop what I would call the Normandy approach of Hollande and Merkel. This is what they want to stop. They were furious against that, against the relative independence of Hollande and Merkel on this.

Papert: The Normandy approach to solution of the Ukraine crisis.

Cheminade: Yes, exactly. The Minsk agreement.

So this started in Normandy. It started before, by the way. It started in Brisbane [in November 2014] when Hollande asked Putin into his car, and said, I want to have a discussion with you. We don't agree, but I want to have a discussion with you. Putin was being boycotted by the other Western powers.

So Hollande is Hollande. He's not a man who has tremendous vision or courage, but in a certain way, he understands where he is. Also, around him is Pierre de Villiers, who's the head of the General Staff of the French Army, who's always in the pictures with him—he's the brother of Philippe de Villiers, a sovereignist,—and Benoit Puga, who is also a general who is the head of the military staff of Hollande. So he's surrounded by military forces, and the military forces are really pissed at what the United States is not doing.

That's what they say.

So you have a very interesting situation, potentially. It should not be underestimated, it shouldn't be overestimated, but it's a definite change, if you compare it to what was going on a few weeks ago, because of what happened in Paris.

Also, the Russians are saying, "We hope that it will be proto-Gaullist, or a type of Gaullist approach again in French foreign policy." So that's also on the table. It has not yet happened, but a potential has appeared. And the French population has to say that they have to organize themselves to defend their idea of the principle of a republic, and they understand quite well that that is what is threatened at this point.

Marianne, for example, is a French publication read by everyone in the government. I'm reading it now. What they say is that this was a sort of French Pearl Harbor, and they add that—I have it here—about Obama, they say of Obama, "he is too full of himself to care for the world." That's a quote.

Papert: [Laughs.] That's very polite.

Cheminade: It doesn't go far enough but as you say, it means that the people around government circles are pissed. They say that America today is an autistic country.

Papert: It's all Obama.

Cheminade: And they believe too much that Europe will do something. But nonetheless, the Europeans—including the French and the Germans, including Merkel and Hollande, who are not great humanists—but they feel that the chair on which they are sitting is about to fall over, and they have to do something.

The Potential

Papert: It's been short but I think very enlightening. Are there other things you think you should say before we close?

Cheminade: Yes. It was the Saudis. What a lot of people are saying now is that: if the Saudis finance al-Sisi, good. If the Saudis fear that Da'esh would go after them, good. If the Saudis buy our planes, good. But if the Saudis want to do something beyond their borders, we have to stop them, if they are playing games.

So, at this point, this is all they are saying, but they are saying it—and the same with Qatar. And Qatar, out of fear, has established certain controls of the financing of the jihadists, of the terrorists. So that, in a sense, is very limited, but it's significant nonetheless.

The main thing is the economic component. As long as there is not a move towards Glass-Steagall—and a lot of people are talking again about Glass-Steagall—and the return of the state against the financial forces, the City of London and Wall Street,—if this doesn't take place, what is potentially positive in what France is doing, will lead nowhere, as it led nowhere after Chirac's opposition to the war against Iraq.

I have to add that a lot of people are looking again at what I had said as the leading point of my presidential campaign, which was "A World Without the City and Without Wall Street." And they are thinking, yes, you were right. This is a world for peace through common development. This is win-win strategy, and this is what is necessary. So there is a rethinking of the whole French policy of the last, let's say 30 years, 40 years.

Papert: Thank you so much.

Obama and the Indonesian Murder Cult

by Mike Billington

Nov. 30—Lyndon LaRouche has demanded that no American elected official, policy-maker, or citizen be allowed to avoid or deny the overwhelming evidence that President Barack Obama is a mass murderer, an individual who kills "for pleasure." LaRouche has also stated that Obama learned how to be a mass murderer from his step-father of fifteen years, Lolo Soetoro, an Indonesian national who took part in the mass genocide against supporters of Indonesian President Sukarno between 1965 and 1966 in Indonesia.

What is less well known is the role played by the Indonesian-based pseudo-religious cult Subud, an organization directly involved in carrying out the Indonesian massacres and an organization to which Barack Obama's mother, Ann Dunham, had very deep ties. Although there is no publicly available paper trail proving that Ann Dunham was a member of the mystical cult Subud, it is known with certainty that she was very closely associated with many of its members, both Indonesians and western members living in Indonesia at that time.

Obama's step-father, Lolo Soetoro, a member of the Indonesian military who was studying at the University of Hawaii at the time, was called back to Indonesia in 1966 by General Suharto, soon after Suharto's coup against the Father of Indonesia's Independence, President Sukarno. This was precisely at the moment that General Suharto was unleashing mass slaughter against Sukarno's supporters. It is well documented that the coup, and the geno-

Bapak Muhammad Subuh Sumohadiwidjojo (1901-1987), founder of the Subud cult.

cide that followed, were orchestrated by the United States, the British, and the Australians, acting through their Ambassadors in Jakarta (see Box, next page).

Soetoro, like all members of Suharto's military regime, would have been called upon to participate in the slaughter, which killed somewhere between 500,000 and a million Indonesian citizens for the "crime" of supporting Sukarno and/or the Indonesian Communist Party (PKI), of being of Chinese descent, or simply of not supporting the military junta. The massacres in Indonesia were barbaric,—some by gun, others by machete, others by other means.

While Obama's step-father was engaged in the military side of this blood-lust, the Subud cult, which his mother became involved in, took part in the civilian mobs that participated in the killing. The founder of Subud, Muhammad Subuh Sumohadiwidjojo (called Bapak, meaning father, by Subud members) was by that time deeply connected to British military intelligence, which had helped to spread his cult internationally. Of even greater importance, Subud was one of the leading institutional supporters of Suharto's coup and participated in the slaughter of the innocents.

Bapak

The biography of Ann Dunham Obama/Soetoro by *New York Times* journalist Janny Scott (*A Singular Woman*) reveals that Dunham, while living in Indonesia with her husband and Barack from 1967-71, was deeply affiliated with members of

U.S., British, and Australian Embassies in Jakarta Orchestrated the Mass Murders of 1965-66

It is clear from cables released in 1999 that the British, the Australians, and the U.S. Embassies in Jakarta played the controlling role in the overthrow of Sukarno in 1965 and the mass slaughter of Sukarno's supporters over 1965 and 1966.

Primary among them was U.S. Ambassador Marshall Green, newly appointed with the explicit assignment to overthrow Sukarno in collaboration with the Indonesian General Suharto. Immediately following the kidnapping and murder of several leading military figures on September 30, The Suharto group, and Amb. Green, declared the attempted military coup to be a communist plot (which it was not), and promoted the subsequent massacre.

Indonesian coup leader Gen. Suharto, with one of his key international sponsors, U.S. Ambassador Marshall Green, in 1965.

Green wired Washington on Oct. 5:

> Muslim groups and others except communists and their stooges are lined up behind army.... Army now has opportunity to move against PKI if it acts quickly.... In short, it's now or never. Much remains in doubt, but it seems almost certain that agony of ridding Indonesia of effects of Sukarno ... has begun.... Spread the story of PKI's guilt, treachery and brutality—This priority effort is perhaps most needed.

Australian Ambassador Sir Mick Shann echoed this sentiment:

> Now or never...; if Sukarno and his greasy civilian cohorts get back into the saddle it will be a change for the worse.... We are dealing with such an odd, devious, contradictory mess like the Indonesian mind.

The British-American-Commonwealth leadership knew of the killing from the beginning. Under the direction of the military, much of the slaughter was carried out by enraged Muslim youth, armed and turned loose against any and all supporters of the Sukarno/PKI programs. We now know that the Subud members participated in the slaughter.

Ambassador Green's cables as early as Oct. 20 referred to hundreds of summary executions, but warned that the PKI was "capable of recovering quickly if ... Army attacks were stopped." He praised the Army for "working hard at destroying PKI and I, for one, have increasing respect for its determination and organization in carrying out this crucial assignment." A cable from the American consul in Medan, in Northeast Sumatra, is most revealing: "Two officers of Pemuda Pantjasila [a Muslim youth group] told consulate officers that their organization intends to kill every PKI member they can catch ..., much indiscriminate killing is taking place.... Attitude Pemuda Pantjasila leaders can only be described as bloodthirsty.... Something like a real reign of terror against PKI is taking place. The terror is not (repeat) not discriminating very carefully between PKI leaders and ordinary PKI members with no ideological bond to the party." He added that there was "no meaningful resistance."

Approximately one-half million Indonesians were murdered in cold blood over the next several months.

Green concluded in his memoirs that "the bloodbath ... can be attributed to the fact that communism, with its atheism and talk of class warfare, was abhorrent to the way of life of rural Indonesians, especially in Java and Bali."

It is coherent with Green's fond embrace of the genocidal "solution" to the problem (as he perceived it), that he went on to become one of the world's leading promoters of population control, setting up population control units in the State Department and the National Security Council, and heading the U.S. delegation to the UN Population Commission.

—*Mike Billington*

See a full report.

Subud, some of whom were her very close personal friends. When setting up an English-language school for a Ford Foundation-funded institution, she hired a group of Subud members, and socialized with them in the evenings. She and one of her closest friends, Mohammad Mansur Medeiros, a leading Subud member, spent so much time together that a fellow teacher, quoted in Dunham's biography, said, "You would think they were in love, but they were not."

There was a major international conference of Subud in the summer of 1971 at their headquarters in Cilandak, a suburb of Jakarta. Many of Ann Dunham's Subud friends were there, and it is quite possible that she and her husband both attended that conference.

Here is where the story coincides with her husband's role in the genocide five years earlier:

An American member of Subud, who had joined the group while living in Southeast Asia for the previous two years, attended the international conference that summer in Cilandak. As he told the story to *EIR*, he was unfamiliar with Subud's history or its political associations, but had joined only because of his interest in the group's spiritual exercises (called the *latihan kejiwaan* in Indonesian).

One evening at the week-long conference, the young American was chatting with a group of older members from Chile, along with several other Americans and a few Indonesians. He asked the Chileans about the election of President Salvador Allende the previous year, 1970. The Chileans very heatedly denounced Allende as a communist who was destroying Chile. The young member had read about Allende and thought he had been doing some positive things for the country, and tried to defend his policies.

The Chilean Subud members became extremely agitated, and, joined by the other Americans and the Indonesians, angrily berated the young American. Finally one of them burst out: "You don't understand. The communists are evil. When the communists were taking over Indonesia, Bapak called on all Subud members to pick up their machetes and help cleanse the country of this evil."

John G. Bennett (1897-1974), head of British Military Intelligence for the Middle East in the 1920s, and a proselytizer for the Subud cult. He is shown with his wife Elizabeth.

Two years later, Allende was murdered in a military coup by Gen. Augusto Pinochet; the murder was followed by a mass killing of communists on the model of the Indonesian slaughter. Pinochet was eventually brought to justice. Suharto and his western sponsors never were.

Subud and Bapak's personal role in backing Suharto is not denied. Indeed, there is a film available on YouTube showing Gen. Suharto visiting Cilandak for the opening of a new Latihan hall during the 1971 international conference, where Suharto fondly greets his friend Bapak.

However, Subud's role in the genocide, as revealed here, has been carefully covered up, not only in Subud's voluminous historical records, but in all other sources as well.

Subandrio, Sukarno's Foreign Minister and close ally, accused Subud and Bapak of being assets of the CIA in their efforts to overthrow Sukarno—as in fact came to pass, and *EIR*'s source confirmed above.

British Military Intelligence

Not surprisingly, there is a very close connection between Subud and British intelligence. In fact, the head of British military intelligence for the Mideast in the 1920s, John G. Bennett, was personally responsible for the spread of Subud internationally in the 1950s. By that time Bennett had become the British intelligence service's leading profiler of the world's various mystical sects.

It all began with the Russian mystic G.I. Gurdjieff and his student P.D. Ouspensky, whom Bennett was assigned to monitor after World War I, when they migrated from Russia to western Europe. Bennett became a leading representative in the UK for the Gurdjieff method of the mystical "Fourth Way" to a higher consciousness. For the next 30 years Bennett taught the Gurdjieff method, while dabbling in other mystical sects along the way. He created his own "Institute for the Comparative Study of History, Philosophy and the Sciences" in the UK in 1946, centered on the Gurdjieff method but bringing together other mystics from around the world—a perfect petri dish for both profiling and manipulating such movements.

In 1956, a member of the Subud movement showed up at Bennett's Institute, and Bennett joined the movement immediately. Bennett quickly arranged for Bapak to come to the UK, and within months was traveling around the world, often with Bapak, spreading the movement. He also translated some of Bapak's writings and wrote a book called *Concerning Subud*.

Soetoro's Killer Profile

The connection of Ann Dunham Soetoro and her husband Lolo to the slaughter of 1965-66 was indirectly revealed in Obama's autobiography *Dreams from My Father*, published in 1995. Obama reports that "something happened between her [his mother] and Lolo in the year that they had been apart"—i.e., the year that Soetoro spent in Indonesia during the genocide, before Dunham and Barack joined him in 1967. "Soetoro had been full of life in Hawaii," wrote Obama, and had told stories of his father and brother fighting and dying in the war for independence from the Dutch after World War II. He had looked forward to returning to Indonesia from the East-West Center at the University of Hawaii to build a new Indonesia.

Back in Indonesia, "He [Soetoro] didn't talk that way any more," Obama wrote. "It was as if he had pulled into some dark hidden place, out of reach. On some nights, she would hear him up after everyone else had gone to bed, wandering through the house with a bottle of imported whiskey, nursing his secrets. Other nights he would tuck a pistol under his pillow before falling off to sleep."

Obama tried to pass this off as due to Soetoro's problems with his job. Dunham's biographer Scott said

he was bothered by the corruption in the military government and the army. The obvious truth is that the nightmares and torment came from his participation in the mass killing. There are many accounts of the fact that military personnel, especially those recalled from foreign studies, such as Lolo Soetoro, had to prove their loyalty by participating directly in the mass killings.

Obama also provides an insight into his stepfather's psychology as a killer, one which is now so apparent in Obama himself. Obama reports the following in praise of his stepfather, and as a major lesson in his life:

> "Have you ever seen a man killed?" I asked him.
> He glanced down, surprised by my question.
> "Have you?" I asked again.
> "Yes," he said.
> "Was it bloody?"
> "Yes."
> I thought for a moment. "Why was the man killed? The one you saw?"
> "Because he was weak."
> "That's all?"
> Lolo shrugged. "That's usually enough. Men take advantage of weakness in other men. They're just like countries in that way. The strong man takes the weak man's land. He makes the weak man work in his fields. If the weak man's woman is pretty, the strong will take her. Which would you rather be?"
> I didn't answer, and Lolo squinted up at the sky. "Better to be strong," he said finally, rising to his feet. "If you can't be strong, be clever and make peace with someone who is strong. But always better be strong yourself. Always."

Obama also reports that Soetoro once told him that "a man took on the powers of whatever he ate. One day soon, he promised, he would bring home a piece of tiger meat for us to share."

Subud Connections

In 1968 Ann Dunham Soetoro renewed her American passport. On the application form, under the section titled "Amend to Include (Exclude) Children," she wrote the name Barack Hussein Obama followed by the name "Soebarkah" in parentheses. That name, Soebarkah, appears nowhere else in Obama's history. Where did it come from?

This passport application came at the time when Ann Dunham was actively involved with Subud, and it is possible that it is a "Subud name" for her son Barack. The source who related to *EIR* the story of his membership in Subud in 1971, also explained that members who met Bapak were often given a Subud name. The member was asked to suggest three names that they would like to have as a Subud name, and Bapak would choose the "correct one" in keeping with the "higher consciousness." Soebarkah sounds like a name Ann and Lolo may have chosen for their Subud son.

Another Subud connection emerged in 2011 in Hawaii. One Loretta Fuddy was appointed Director of the Hawaii Department of Health in 2011, and it was this same Loretta Fuddy who thereafter released Barack Obama's supposed Hawaii Certificate of Live Birth—a document which was a subject of great controversy and secrecy both before and after its release by Fuddy.

Loretta Fuddy was a leading member of Subud, serving as chairwoman of Subud's U.S.A. National Committee from 2006-8. Her Subud name was Deliana. She died in a plane crash in 2013, although all the other passengers in the crash survived.

Removal of Obama from Office

It is now clear to the world, as Lyndon LaRouche has insisted for years, that Barack Obama is a killer, taking great pride in his bombing of several nations into oblivion, nations which posed no threat to the United States,—leaving them in the hands of warring terrorist factions, and driving their population into frantic and dangerous escape from the terrorists as refugees. He delights in drawing up his weekly kill list, as if he were a feudal king, deciding who shall die this week through drone assassination, with no due process or recourse to protest the death sentence, or that of whatever family members and friends happen to be there at the time. He has publicly bragged that if there is one thing he is good at, it is "killing people." The stench from the massacres carried out by his stepfather and the Subud friends of his mother lives on today in the mind of their son. It is a psychotic killer mentality.

It is time for Obama's impeachment, or to apply the 25th Amendment of the U.S. Constitution to remove him from office, before he carries out his current threat to launch a thermonuclear war on Russia.

EIR Reconstruction Proposal Receives Unprecedented Attention in Syria

by Ulf Sandmark

Nov. 30—From November 14-22, 2015, Helga Zepp-La-Rouche's Schiller Institute brought a proposal directly into Syria for immediately starting reconstruction of that war-ravaged nation. The plan, published in the Nov. 13 edition of *EIR*, received extensive attention within leading institutions and media, showing the eagerness of that nation for such a reconstruction effort. Clearly a broad mobilization for reconstruction like the one that the Institute proposed—one led by the establishing of a national reconstruction bank, utilizing the most modern technology, and linking Syria with great infrastructure projects of the great New Silk Road development projects—is possible.

EIRNS/Ulf Sandmark

The Swedish delegation meets with Patriarch Ignatius Aphrem II. Reporter Ulf Sandmark is shown speaking to the Patriarch.

A fifteen-person delegation from the Swedish NGO Syrian Support Committee for Democracy took the Schiller plan, called Phoenix Project Syria, to Damascus. The delegation included this author, an economist from the Schiller Institute and *EIR*'s Stockholm correspondent.

The Swedish NGO is one of the best-known Syrian exile organizations supporting Syria today. It is pushing for re-establishment of diplomatic relations and an end to the murderous EU embargo. The delegation was able to meet with Dr. Bouthaina Shaaban, the political and media advisor to the President of Syria, Bashar al-Assad, and also with Prime Minister Wael al-Halqi and four ministries. Meetings also occurred with the Speaker of the Parliament; the chairmen of the al-Baath party, both internationally and nationally; and the three top religious leaders of Syria,—the Grand Mufti of Syria, Dr. Badr al-Din Hasson, who made a point of receiving the delegation together with the Bishop of the Greek Orthodox Church, Lukas al-Khouri; and the Patriarch of the Syrian Orthodox Church, Ignatius Aphrem II.

Patriarch Aphrem was already acquainted with Alexander Hamilton, upon whose work the Schiller Institute proposal heavily relies. Before his assumption of leadership of all of international Syrian Orthodoxy, Aphrem had been its bishop based in New Jersey, U.S.A.

The delegation also held discussions with leaders of several national aid organizations, including the Chairwoman of the national aid organization al-Waed, Rim Suleiman; Mother Agnes Miriam and her aid organization; the Executive Director of St. Ephrem Patriarchical

Development Committee, Shadi Sarweh; the Chairwoman of the National Family Organization (FAM); a Board member from The Syria Trust for Development, Talal Moualla; and the Chairman of the National organization of Medical Doctors. Two military rehabilitation hospitals were visited, at the invitation of the Surgeon General of the Syrian Army, Dr. Moriss Mowaz.

In all meetings the *EIR* article "Phoenix Project Syria: Discussion Points on Syrian Reconstruction" was briefly presented, in addition to the Arabic language translation.

Upon my return, I answered a series of questions from *EIR*, presented below:

EIR: Was there a formal press conference or presentation of the report?

Sandmark: At the agency responsible for reconstruction, the Syrian Investment Agency, I gave a presentation on the proposal to the General Director, Engineer Hala Ghazal, and her staff, as well as assembled journalists.

I described the creation of a Syrian Phoenix Reconstruction bank as an opportunity for Syria to kickstart rebuilding, and unite the nation. A credit system could finance the urgent necessity of putting all available unemployed labor to work in reconstruction and development. This would be especially important because it would make it possible to reconcile former rebels by bringing them into a common effort for the nation, and also to recruit back the very much missed youth who have gone abroad as refugees.

As the reconstruction proposal had been presented to this audience before our trip, my presentation stressed what was not known—how the Western world had adopted just such a dirigist economic policy during emergencies such as wars and depressions. Throughout the Third World and Eastern Europe, nations are only allowed to apply Western monetarist economics, such as now dominates every university, and are forced to submit to conditionalities for national reconstruction of the sort concocted by the IMF, World Bank, and the Western financial institutions.

The Schiller Institute proposal was enthusiastically received by both officials and some journalists. The major question during the many discussions during the visit was: Will they allow us to do this? However, when we pointed to the new paradigm of the BRICS, who are already working according to these economic principles, that was enough to reassure the questioner.

As the Syrian Investment Agency is open to immediately starting some projects, we discussed several Swedish private reconstruction projects to begin immediately; this would start to break the embargo. A joint working group was also suggested, which would involve Syrians refugees in Sweden and others who want to start planning a reconstruction project in Syria. Mapping would be needed to find out what kind of education and vocational training will be needed, and how the refugees can be brought into such education programs and job training.

Similar preparations would be necessary to identify the different industries and research institutes that have relevant technology for Syrian reconstruction and, in general, for the development of the whole New Silk Road. Studies and planning of all aspects of the New Silk Road and models of the Phoenix Reconstruction Bank would also begin, with the intention to spread such activities in organizations in Sweden. Each organization for each profession needs to start a working group, so that all aspects of the great New Silk Road Project can be mapped out; in this context, necessary attention can be paid to Syria as a very important transport node in the Silk Road network.

EIR: Can you give us more of an idea of the content of your discussions with the religious leaders, both informal and formal—and with other people you were able to discuss with?

Sandmark: The proposal for a Reconstruction Bank and a credit system was also discussed with the religious leaders. Actually they were the ones who could most easily see the moral dimension of creating credit "out of nothing" for realizing the great potentials of Syria. I picked up on this and emphasized the moral aspect in every subsequent presentation by noting that this economic policy is self-evident for a religious person. Just ask yourself: Should God have waited for the money, when he created the world out of nothing?

I also raised the issue of climate, as this now is being posed as a religious issue after the tragic mistake of the Pope, and left them with the *EIR* Special Report "Global Warming Scare Is Population Reduction, Not Science."

EIR: You say there was lots of media coverage. Can you tell us more about its content, headlines? Was it TV, newspapers, radio?

Sandmark: The meetings were covered for five days in a row on TV. More and more the coverage, which was also massive in newspapers, took up the idea of a Phoenix Reconstruction bank.

The TV coverage included three 50 minute interviews on Al-Ikhbaria and Al-Talaki, where members of the delegation spoke in Arabic about the activities in support of Syria in Sweden, but also about the idea of a Reconstruction bank and the New Silk Road policies. One of the hosts of the TV programs said that the interview he just did, was the best and most interesting he had done in his whole career.

EIR: What is the impact of the embargo on the Syrian people?

Sandmark: The most vicious impact of the EU/UN embargo is on the health sector, where it has had murderous effects. Humanitarian aid is supposed to be allowed under the embargo, but our visit to the Minister of Health, Dr. Nizar Yazigi, demonstrated that the West is not living up to such humanitarian duties. There is a lack of medicine, especially for long-term illnesses like cancer and diabetes. People with such illnesses just die if they do not get the medicines they require, which are smuggled into the country surreptitiously and at great expense.

The Minister described how every citizen of Syria still gets all medical treatment and the available medicines for free. This is despite the targeting of the pharmaceutical factories by the terrorists, who dismantled them, sold equipment to Turkey, and left them destroyed. New factories have been built, and with the help of Russia and Iran, Syria is now getting 89 percent of its needed medical supplies. Pharmacies in areas occupied by the terrorists are supplied with drugs by the government. The Minister proudly said that the nation has so far avoided any epidemics.

The 1200-bed Tishreen Military Hospital in Damascus was built by the French and has now been destroyed by terrorists. Half of its doctors were trained in France. Because most of the hospital equipment is from Europe, the embargo is very damaging to Syria in spite of words about allowing humanitarian aid. When machines are broken, they cannot be repaired. Spare parts smuggled via Jordan are sold at twice the normal price. As there are no medical instruments available from Russia, the aid from there and from Iran cannot solve these problems.

The World Health Organization helps with some of the things Syria lacks, and UNICEF supplies some children's medicines, but when asked about the Red Cross, the staff of the Health ministry said bluntly that "that is a political organization;" it only supplies those it likes.

Dr. Bouthaina Shaaban, the political and media advisor to Syrian President Bashar Assad, talking with state TV, after her meeting with the Swedish delegation.

The staffers said that nothing has been delivered to the government health sector from the Red Cross. However, often the nutritional special biscuits for children, supplied by the Red Cross, have been found in the possession of the terrorists.

EIR: Can you give us a sense of how people see the Russian intervention, whether people believe that ISIS can be defeated, and how they view Obama's personal role?

Sandmark: Dr. Bouthaina Shaaban started by explaining that she knows why the Western media and the TV stations Al-Jazeera and Al-Arabiya are lying. She got the shock treatment when meeting with State Department official William Burns and Elliott Abrams in Washington. After listening to Burns for a while, she dared to interrupt him saying: "Sorry, what you are saying is not relevant to the Syrian situation." To which Burns exclaimed: "Who cares about relevance? It's concepts!"

"Syria was the only Arab country against the NATO invasion of Libya. Where is the news about Libya today?" Dr. Shabaan asked. "Who speaks about Yemen? What did the Yemen people do? How can the West be silent about Yemen, as if on another planet? Of 19 hijackers on 9-11, 17 were from Saudi Arabia! We lost a lot. But the West lost its credibility among the Arab people." ... "They look at us as colonies and we take that into account."

She continued: "London embraced the Muslim Brotherhood. Most of the leaders those fighting in Syria

Some unreconstructed suburbs of Damascus

EIRNS/Ulf Sandmark

are foreigners. They do not even show their faces to others while eating. It was when Russia heard the terrorists spoke Russian among themselves that they decided to intervene to defend their security in Syria. ... The terrorists will have to leave. We've had many occupiers. They either die or leave. Syria will prevail."

Confidence in the government and the support by the Russians was visible in the decreased level of fear in the population, shown by more people in the streets in the evenings, compared to our last visit one year ago. The delegation was able to move into many more districts in Damascus, including areas that were closed to us last year. People are repairing the damage from the war as rapidly as possible. Going around by car, I tried to find any traces of the war, but they were nowhere to be seen in central Damascus and in the suburbs. Only in Eastern Ghouta, in the suburbs along the airport road, could I see war-damaged housing districts, but even those were under repair.

The military was disciplined and well-dressed in their Syrian-made uniforms and proceeded efficiently with their controls at the many military checkpoints in the city. The war was only heard at a distance from time to time, especially in the morning hours. On Thursday, Nov. 19th, when the terrorists took revenge against the Syrian army for killing three terrorist leaders in different places in Syria, Damascus was hit by 37 mortar shells, which killed and injured many ordinary citizens. The next day we saw that the damage had been cleaned up, and that people were going about their business in the same streets; this is a fully functioning capital city and home front.

EIR: Do you have anything else to add?

Sandmark: Yes, I would like to add an observation about something I had not expected to find so strong, even though, in retrospect, I should have expected it in a country with institutions thousands of years old. What I noted was that there is continuous discussion about such important cultural matters as the Nature of God (and therefore also of Man). I should have known, since Syria is already in a dialogue with China about their respective thousands of years of philosophical and cultural evolution.

I concluded that the dialogue on reconstruction is ready to become a dialogue of civilizations. Leading people in Syria are working to define a concept of nationhood from the highest standpoint of their very rich cultural heritage. This is part of a deep-going reaction against Islamic fundamentalism and a surge in the population for old values. We could see clearly, compared to last year, that now the Syrian flag is held up much more by the government to represent the nation. We could see that Syria is presented much more as a country where all groups with their many thousands of years-old cultures tolerate and live together. The ancient heritage monuments do not only represent the past but also the future Syria. It means that there is now a genuine openness for a dialogue of civilizations on the highest universal values, like those of Schiller.

In this way, the most efficient ideological counteroffensive against the barbaric ideas of ISIS can get underway, and also help Western countries find the weaknesses in their own cultures that allowed their countries to be used as a staging grounds for so many terrorists that were sent to attack Syria.

World Forum on China Studies Focuses on China's New Global Role

by William Jones

Nov. 29—The World Forum on China Studies, held on November 20-21, is a biannual event sponsored by the Shanghai Academy of Social Studies, which this year brought together some three hundred of the most prominent Sinologists from China and from around the world. While the forum always encompasses a broad range of topics, from philosophy, to economics, to social studies. This year's gathering was particularly noteworthy in its focus on the Chinese project of the Silk Road Economic Belt and the Maritime Silk Road. The theme for this years conference was "China's Reform—Opportunities For the World."

The rapid growth of the Chinese economy as the primary motor of world-wide development over the course of the last decades has thrust it into a major role on the global stage, a role for which there is no clear road-map. And contrary to what neo-conservatives in the West would like people to believe, there is no secret "plot" by China to take over the world. Given the shape of the world as we know it today, no individual nation would willingly take upon itself such a monumental task, particularly not a nation like China, with its long tradition of Confucian harmony. China, also, still has a long way to go to raise up the 300,000,000 of their own people who are still living in poverty.

And yet, this rapidly growing international role of

William Jones/EIRNS

Yu Yunquan, the Deputy Director of the Center for International Communication Studies at China International Publishing Group, addresses the Shanghai World Forum on China Studies.

China is not, as some blithe spirits might envision, a matter of China simply "integrating" into the "western" economic system as we know it—a system which has long been ripe for the scrap heap. While China has "westernized" in some respects, it represents a distinctly different culture from the Western world, and it is this cultural matrix above all which will determine the road China will take in the global arena. And this, in turn, will have a dramatic effect on the shape of the world as a whole.

This notion was quite clearly summarized at the end of the Forum by Yang Shuang, Deputy Director General of the Publicity Department of the Shanghai Chinese Communist Party. He noted three sources from which China will develop its "China Path": from traditional Chinese culture, particularly the Confucian tradition; from Marxism; and from the last thirty years' "reform and opening," the policy initiated by Deng Xiaoping.

Most profoundly, there is the Confucian tradition. While this has often been depicted as being "anti-modern" (criticized in the wake of the 1911 Revolution) or anti-socialist (repressed during the period of the Cultural Revolution), Confucianism's underlying presence in Chinese culture over the last 1500 years has been deep and long-lasting. And it has been clearly and decisively revived by the present leadership of China as an active and vital element in the rejuvenation of the Chinese nation.

Intertwined with this millennia-long influence of Confucian culture, is the reality of the Chinese experience with Marxism. While the doctrines of Karl Marx have long since disappeared from the horizon in the debates in the West, Marxism remains to this day a major factor in China's development, serving still as the basic orientation of the Chinese Communist Party, the key actor in China's development. In today's China, that Marxist outlook is expressed in the Chinese doctrines of raising the masses out of poverty and misery, and in the important role that the state plays in providing a directionality for the overall economy, albeit now, in an economy where individual initiative is beginning to play a more important role. Marxism is also a major factor in creating a sense of obligation among the party cadre to work for the benefit of the working masses.

In the developing reality of today's China, these two elements—Confucianism and Marxism—intertwine in a very interesting manner, as seen, for instance, in the concept of the "peoples livelihood," a concept made popular by Dr. Sun Yatsen, the founder of modern China. However, Dr. Sun's notion can already be found in a variety of forms in the classical Confucian works, characterized particularly by the notion of the "mandate of heaven."

Finally, among those influences shaping current Chinese policy, there is the experience of Deng Xiaopeng's "reform and opening up." Yang Shuang noted that next year will be the 30th anniversary of the initiation of the "reform and opening up" initiative. This policy of "opening up" will continue, but at a pace and in a form which will be monitored and regulated by the party and the government. And it will serve to enhance China's role in contributing to the world at large. "Our commitment comes from our dedication to world civilization," Yang said. "We are committed to reduce poverty in China and in the world."

Yang Shuang also noted that there was a crying need for more Chinese scholars to become involved in "China Studies" in order to better explain China to the world. While "China Studies" has been something of a favorite theme in the West since it was initiated by the Jesuits during the Seventeenth Century, it is of relatively new vintage for many Chinese scholars. But with the emergence of China as a major player in the international arena, this has now become an urgent need in order to avoid serious misunderstandings regarding China, its goals, and its intentions.

'Please Don't Misread China'

Speaking to the opening banquet of the conference on November 20th, Fu Ying, director of the Foreign Affairs Committee of the National People's Congress, underlined the importance of the rest of the world coming to understand China. "Please don't misread China," she said. This is the 70th anniversary of the end of World War II, she said, and the world is once again experiencing the winds of change.

Fu Ying noted that much of the Western commentary on China was often based on prejudice and arrogance, something that she hoped might be avoided. Our system and our cultures are different, she said, but they are not contradictory. The key element for scholars, both Chinese and Western, is to find the means for explaining to the world, in an understandable way, China's desires and intentions. "Constructing a completely effective narrative is a need of our times," she said. "The Chinese narrative must also resolve the huge errors in the understanding abroad of China, utilizing a more

FIGURE 1

A Chinese schematic of the New Silk Road/One Belt One Road outreach to the world.

systematic and faultless theory, using a more straight-forward and persuasive language, allowing the outside world to better understand and trust us in order to achieve the '200 year goal' of building a more peaceful and stable external environment." She also urged the foreign scholars to read the works of Chinese scholars more in order to get a better sense of Chinese thinking.

There was also a considerable participation in the conference by scholars from many other countries: from Asia, from Europe, from Africa, from Latin America, and from the United States. There was much enthusiasm over the possibilities opened up by the Silk Road project. Representatives from Peru and Argentina, from Mongolia, South Africa, and Pakistan waxed eloquent in their praise of China's role in launching the "Belt and Road" perspective.

A speech by this author in one of the round-tables on the Belt and Road as a "New Paradigm for Mankind," in contrast to the threatening specter of nuclear war now on the horizon, was well-received by the other participants. Also scholars from Japan, including a former Japanese ambassador to the United Nations, gave speeches praising the Chinese development policies and lamenting the fact that, under the present Abe regime, Japan has become a tool for those right-wing circles in the United States who hope to use Japan as a marcher-lord for their imperial ambitions.

Several scholars were given awards for their contributions to China studies, including the venerable Russian China scholar, Mikhail Titarenko, one of the founders of modern China Studies in Russia and a good friend of American economist and statesman Lyndon LaRouche. While Titarenko's health did not permit him to

participate this year, he did send his greetings in a video addressed to the conference participants.

The appeal for greater understanding of China, its goals and its wishes, expressed by numerous speakers, should not be misinterpreted, however, simply as that of a "supplicant" seeking "understanding" from a more powerful compatriot. Chinese scholars are keenly aware of the fact that the attitude of the present Obama regime, while cordial on the surface, is far from friendly. They are aware that the Obama Administration is largely motivated by an attempt to re-establish the Cold War order with a vengeance, a policy which is dangerously close to heating up into nuclear conflict. Yet, they remain confident of their ability to lead China in the direction they intend to go, regardless of any threats or external pressures.

While rejecting any wild notions of becoming a "hegemonic" power, a myth which is continually perpetrated in the Western press, they are demanding that they be given their rightful place in the political order now that they have become the most important player in the economic order. If the Western nations do not accede to this justified demand, the consequences can be devastating for the world.

Ironically, doing the "right thing" in this case is also the only way for the Western nations to create a brighter future for themselves. A new world economic order based on the notions imbuing China's "Road and Belt" is the only way out of the dilemma caused by the collapse of the dollar-based financial system.

Most of the developing world has already recognized this fact, as we have seen in the tremendous support garnered for the "Belt and Road" from the nations of Africa and Latin America. The people of the United States deserve better, and if they would take it upon themselves to move rapidly for the impeachment of Obama, the single impediment to joining the"Belt and Road" and whose crimes against humanity are clear for all to see, they would also serve to benefit from the new perspective offered by China's rejuvenation, which then could become a "rejuvenation" of the world economy transforming the infrastructural investment policies of the Silk Road Economic Belt into a World Landbridge.

Every Day Counts In Today's Showdown To Save Civilization

That's why you need EIR's **Daily Alert Service**, a strategic overview compiled with the input of Lyndon LaRouche, and delivered to your email 5 days a week.

For example: On November 5, EIR's Daily Alert featured Lyndon LaRouche's warning that Obama can and must be removed immediately, to avoid Obama's push for thermonuclear confrontation with Russia. That issue identified The Drone Papers put out by Glenn Greenwald's The Intercept as the Pentagon Papers of 2015—damning Barack Obama as a mass murderer, and providing the evidence for his Constitutional removal from office.

That edition also featured EIR's exclusive report on a hearing called by Rep. John Conyers on Capitol Hill to expose the dangers represented by Obama's actions—a hearing all but suppressed by other media.

This is intelligence you need to act on, if we are going to survive as a nation and a species. Can you really afford to be without it?

THURSDAY, NOVEMBER 5, 2015

EIR Daily Alert Service

EIR DAILY ALERT SERVICE P.O. BOX 17390, WASHINGTON, DC 20041-0390

- Dump Obama Now or Face Thermonuclear Holocaust
- Extraordinary Capitol Hill Event Warns of Obama Thermonuclear War Provocations against Russia
- Rep. Tulsi Gabbard: Unlawful for U.S. To Wage War in Syria
- Satanic Environmentalist Offensive Launched in U.S.
- O'Malley Campaign Support Grows in Iowa, Key Democrats Say
- Behind the New York Times Headlines on 'Death in Middle Age'
- QE Inflated Wall Street, Screwed Main Street—Says Wall Street
- Russian Defense Ministry Coordinating with Syrian Opposition against ISIS
- Frontex: Arrest Illegal Immigrants!
- Bavaria Considering a Constitutional Case against Merkel
- U.S.-Russian Communications Test over Syria
- Malaysia and ASEAN Stand Up To Obama's Threats over South China Sea
- Barenboim's Orchestra Plays Mozart for Peace in the Middle East

EDITORIAL

Dump Obama Now or Face Thermonuclear Holocaust

✂

Now That Obama Has Brought Us To the Brink of Thermonuclear War

Below is an edited transcript of Lyndon LaRouche's Nov. 28 dialog with the Manhattan Project

Dennis Speed: My name is Dennis Speed and on behalf of the LaRouche Political Action Committee, I'd like to welcome you here today. I'm going to start today with a statement that's just been released by Mr. LaRouche. It's entitled "Put Obama Under Lock and Key To Avert Immediate Danger of Nuclear War." The release begins:

"Lyndon H. LaRouche today reiterated, with added urgency, his previous warning that U.S. President Barack Obama is on a determined path toward nuclear war and must be removed from office immediately. The warning comes in response to the escalation of Obama's ongoing nuclear confrontation policy towards Russia as exemplified by the shooting down of a Russian jet over Syria by NATO member and U.S. ally Turkey. The Turkish action could only have occurred with the blessing of Obama. LaRouche's warnings are underscored by assessments of security experts in the U.S. Yet, there is a foolish reluctance among these experts to demand the one remedy that can pull the world back from the threat of nuclear war—removing Obama from control of the U.S. nuclear forces, by impeachment or the activation of the 25th Amendment to the U.S. Constitution.

"The latest warning about possible imminent nuclear war was just published in *Politico Magazine* by a former nuclear-missile launch officer, Bruce G. Blair, titled, "Could U.S.-Russia Tensions Go Nuclear?" Blair points to the Obama Administration's launch-on-warning policy and the shortening of the response time for making a decision about launching nuclear forces. He states that this puts the world on a nuclear hair-trigger more dangerous than during the Cold War.

"Blair warns:

That's especially true since the public doesn't realize just how little time exists for our leaders to make a decision to use nuclear weapons, even today—and if anything, the atmosphere has

U.S. Navy

The testing of the U.S. Aegis destroyer, the USS Shiloh, in June 2006. Deployment of these ships in the Black Sea poses what analyst Bruce Blair called a "decapitation threat" to Moscow.

become even more hair trigger with the threat of cyberwarfare. A launch order is the length of a tweet. Missile crews in turn transmit a short stream of computer signals that immediately ignite the rocket engines of many hundreds of land-based missiles. For the United States, this takes 1 minute. As a former nuclear-missile launch officer, I personally practiced it hundreds of times. We were called Minutemen. U.S. submarine crews take a little longer; they can fire their missiles in 12 minutes.

Enter the Manhattan Project

Blair further elaborates and goes on—I'm not going to read all of it—

Given the 11- to 30-minute flight times of attacking missiles (11 for submarines lurking off the other side's coasts, and 30 for rockets flying over the poles to the other side of the planet), nuclear decision-making under launch on warning—the process from warning to decision to action—is extremely rushed, emotionally charged, and *pro forma*, driven by checklists. I describe it as the rote enactment of a prepared script. In some scenarios, after only a 3-minute assessment of early warning data, the U.S. President receives a 30-second briefing on his nuclear response options and their consequences. He then has a few minutes—12 at most, more likely 3 to 6—to choose one.

"In that context, Obama's deployment of U.S. and allied forces against Russia can only be seen as an escalation towards nuclear conflict. For example, Blair cites the deployment of U.S. Aegis destroyers in the Black Sea armed with cruise missiles that could strike Moscow in minutes. Or the deployment of U.S. strategic bombers flying toward Russia. This, in turn, forces Russia into an escalatory response.

"Blair asks:

Do U.S. leaders understand that the Russians may fear a decapitation threat is emerging, and that this threat may be the underlying driver raising the stakes for Russia to the level of an existential threat warranting preparations for the use of nuclear weapons? I doubt they do.

"The frightening conclusion that Blair does not draw, however, is that U.S. President Barack Obama does know, and intends to create an existential crisis for Russia, and thus, bring the world to the brink of thermonuclear war. Since the beginning of Barack Obama's Presidency, LaRouche has warned that Obama is a narcissistic killer. Everything that Obama has done since has proven LaRouche right. One need only look at Obama's assumption of the role of global executioner, presiding over the regular Tuesday sessions where he personally decides the kill lists for U.S. drone attacks. Or, his confrontational behavior towards Russia in the wake of the Turkish downing of the Russian fighter jet.

"There is no time or room for a long debate on this matter. Obama's nuclear war provocation poses a threat to the existence of the human race. He must be removed now. A single Congressman can initiate impeachment proceedings. Responsible officials within the Presidency can initiate the 25th Amendment on the basis that a President intending to provoke nuclear war is no longer fit for office. The American people must now heed LaRouche's warning. Remove Obama Now!"

And that is the conclusion of the statement.

So, Lyn, I'd like to ask, do you wish to make any further remarks before we begin?

Lyndon LaRouche: No, I think what we said so far on the record, when people assimilate what has been just presented to them, is enough warning for them to pay attention.

Speed: Yes. And I'd just like to say on my own part, when you come to the microphone, come and ask questions—we had a bit of an incident last week of someone filibustering New-Left-style; and we would not only appreciate it, we're going to demand that we stay on topic. We realize that this confrontation with reality might be a bit much for some of the people, some of you who are here for the first time in particular, but let's go and let's confront reality.

Q: Good afternoon, Mr. LaRouche. This is Jessica from Brooklyn. What I want to say has to do with your latest writing, where you said that we must, when we go to interventions or when we go to these events,—I'm particularly concerned about that, when we go to events where we are intervening into a situation where there's an audience; and sometimes the audience is pretty intelligent, sometimes they're not. But we're intervening into the situation where the panel is talking nonsense; and you're saying to humiliate and degrade those people who refuse to say the truth and get the audience to think about educating themselves. I think I got that right.

I want to talk about an incident that happened, and then I'd like you to talk a little more about how we are, or give us ideas about how to actually do that. What we should do as activists in those situations.

You have to Terrify Them

I went to a meeting called "The Important East-West Committee" this past week, and they had a panel of people who were talking about Russia being our ally in the past, the things that need to be done to bring us into cooperation with Russia now. They talked all about how—they knew that Obama had done certain things that were not quite right. Putin had introduced a process of fighting ISIS; Obama really did not sit down with him and go through the things that needed to be done.

This is what they're saying. They knew that there were Nazis in Ukraine; they knew that regime change had taken place. They also knew that a peace process must take place, cooperation must happen. So they said a lot of things that are absolutely true; they also talked about the 50 or troops that were sent into Syria, and that Obama maybe should not have done that.

And the last thing that they said, that really kind of pissed me off (excuse the expression), they said that the strategic intent of Putin was in question.

So when I got a chance to speak, I said, "The strategic intent of *Obama* is what is in question. And Obama has done these things which you have said, and yet, you still haven't seen that you are supposed to impeach him. You're still dancing around, talking about how you're going to 'persuade' him: Well, what're you going to do? You're going to 'persuade' to do better? We're going to talk to him about coming into cooperation with Putin?"

And I said, "Well, the thing that I see as the President, you act like he's just a man, he's just Obama. He may be cute, he may play basketball, you know, all these things. But we're talking about the Presidency, the leader of the United States of America. So what we really should do, when we're talking about our President, and not 'some guy' who you'd like to persuade to do something, is *impeach* him!"

So I challenge the panel to impeach Obama, and I tell the audience, "we must impeach him."

So I hadn't even realized at the time that I talked about his little basketball thing, that Bill Bradley was on the panel! I found out later, and I had a good laugh. But you know, I have been told that that type of thing, where you strike them and humiliate them and degrade them, and make them think about their lives, and also reach the audience. So if you could talk about how we could do more of that, what is the strategy for that? How we as activists have to make that happen, and change people's minds through humor, or if you can get that in, and challenge them to really think, on both the panel and the audience.

LaRouche: It will not work unless you can strike a blow which terrifies them: not in the sense of terrorizing them, but prompting them to realize that they have no option to live, if they don't act on it. And that's the only way it works.

Of course, the people who are going to make the argument have to present a competent case for the argument. They have to point out the initial facts which have to be considered. They have to make a conclusive argument which people have to recognize as being a conclusive argument; otherwise it doesn't work. And therefore, people who are saying "maybe, maybe, maybe...,"

Unsurvivable

A dark, gruesome, but wholly true depiction of the threat of thermonuclear war, its consequences, and Obama's deployment of a major portion of the U.S. thermonuclear capabilities in multiple theaters threatening both Russia and China.

http://larouchepac.com/unsurvivable

maybe these people do not have much of a long period of life-span. And it's people who really can come frankly to the point of decision who're the only ones who are likely survivors in a struggle like this.

Q: [follow-up] OK. So we still have to hit them with the truth of the matter, and at this point, because it's so crucial, we have to reach the terror inside them, to make them think that something has to be done right now.

LaRouche: Yes. And I can deliver any number of accurate messages which will go right directly to that point. My list of indictments of Obama may not be completed, but believe me, it's immense.

Q: Elliot Greenspan: Hi Lyn! I want to pick up where Jessica left off; we were together at this meeting on Monday night at NYU. And I appreciate what she's getting at, and I raise this in part for the assembled here, because what she's done is exemplary in terms of what we need our growing pool of the LaRouche party, of LaRouche activists in New York to do.

Suzanne put together a roster for this week, of about 30 or 40 more possible interventions, and I take your emphasis of a few days ago, when you said we have to move to humiliate Obama, and to denounce everyone who protects Obama within the Congress or within the institutions, or within the population,— and this has to be done now; not two weeks from now. Because the dynamic strategically is in flux.

Obama's Weapon is Fear

What struck me in this meeting, and what I'm getting at in this regard, is that our army here, our activists, have to take immediately greater and greater responsibility. What struck me is the authority which we've got when we come before these poobahs, these great authorities. I made a mistake, when—I went right up to the microphone first, as soon as they made their presentations, but I gave them too much credit.

I was working off of their appearance in the Congressional forum a couple of weeks earlier, before John Conyers, Walter Jones, and others, where we were extremely happy that these guys—two former Ambassadors; former Senator Bradley; Stephen Cohen, the Russian expert; and so on—they appeared before the Congress, and they said to the Congress, "Look, we're facing war with Russia, a new Cold War. This can become nuclear war." And they invoked the Cuban Missile Crisis.

So I began and said, "This is very important what you've done; however, the implication of a new Cold War, Cold Wars can become hot wars. A hot war with Russia is nuclear war, nuclear World War III. Is it not time to invoke the Constitutional remedy to remove Obama before that occurs? Is it not time for the United States to join with the BRICS countries and get rid of British imperial geopolitics, so as to avoid war?"

And the response from these guys—one of them, Ambassador vanden Heuvel, said "Look, what you're raising on impeachment is important; we do have to contain the Executive Branch." But Cohen proceeds to say, as Jessica mentioned, Cohen says, "We're not going to impeach; we'll try to persuade Obama." And Bradley said, "Why are you attacking Obama? He's much better with the Russians than Clinton and Bush." And so on, and so forth.

We approached Cohen at the end and said, "Wait a second, you're talking about a new Cold War, you know where that's going." And we said, "If it's a hot war with Russia, that's nuclear war!" We said, "What does that mean?" He said, "Nuclear war." And yet he would not touch the question of going after Obama in the way that you've done over these years. So, I'm saying, it's crucial for people here to recognize the quality of authority, the unique authority, which we have earned over these years, and which we bring into this Manhattan Project.

But, otherwise, my real question to you is, insofar as these guys, who might be among the best people— Cohen says, "I'm an American patriot for national security"; I mean, they're serious people, from the Roosevelt outlook and so on. And yet, they would not "go there" on the Obama question, or the BRICS question. So, my question is, any elaboration you can give to all of us, in terms of really escalating against them over these days ahead?

LaRouche: Obama's weapon is terror of the victims. The victims include the people who are prominent officials of the U.S. government, and associated with similarly qualified credentials. They are deadly afraid that they are the next one to be killed.

Now, all you have to do to understand about why people are afraid of what Obama's rage might be. It's already shown in the way he has *killed* people, *en masse*, from week to week throughout his career. He's a mass murderer of Representatives of Congress, or anybody else who gets in his way. You have newspapers which are afraid of Obama. The *New York Times* is *ter-*

> **Therefore, you've got two things: You've got the choice of giving in to Obama in order to be killed; or, to be killed by Obama in any case. So, therefore, when you're in a war like that, you don't worry about whether you get in danger or not. What you have to do, is put the cause of the problem into effective danger, which means Obama has to be removed forcibly from office. That is the only thing that will impress the members of Congress to stand up against Obama: that they decided they are going to terrify Obama.**

rified by the very voice of Obama! Leading members of the *New York Times* are *terrified* of doing something which really strongly offends Obama.

Therefore, you've got two things: You've got the choice of giving into Obama in order to be killed; or, to be killed by Obama in any case. So, therefore, when you're in a war like that, you don't worry about whether you get in danger or not. What you have to do, is put the cause of the problem into effective danger, which means Obama has to be removed *forcibly* from office. That is the only thing that will impress the members of Congress to stand up against Obama: that they decided they are going to terrify Obama.

That's where we are. You cannot win this fight unless you are willing to play with the right marbles. And most people are not prepared to understand the problem of the right marbles. We can do it! Obama hates me, probably more than any other person on this planet. And my advice is, I think, the best advice available. He's going to try to kill us, but we're going to get him first, if he tries to make an action. We'll remove him from office. We'll put him in a comfortable place, where he can be tortured by just looking at the walls. [applause]

Why did They Lay Down Their Lives?

Q: Hi, Lyn! It's Alvin, here in New York. On the Thursday call, time wouldn't allow me, after my report on an intervention, to raise what I want to talk with you about now. And it's something that occurred to me on Wednesday.

You know, you get reports, you have a sense of what's being done here in Manhattan, as something that should echo throughout the country as one organization. And I've been fairly involved in that. But it's funny how you think you know something, and you think you're doing something, and then something happens to tell you that you're actually not. And that to me is what the unprovoked attack of Turkey against the Russian jet did. Because I realized that, while we're

doing some good things, I personally have been dancing around the attack that Obama has *always* deserved, has deserved for years, and merely referenced, and not led with it. And that doesn't work.

You've been calling this all along, but it's not until I really felt those missiles on my butt, that I started to realize that. And I don't think I'm special; I think this is going on in other places with other people who are otherwise doing good things, but are not confronting this.

My entire tone, in conversation with any contacts that I have since then, is being directed at that, in no uncertain terms. As far as interventions go, I haven't had too much problem being sarcastic and humiliating; I kind of like that. But when it comes to *talking* to people, I've been dancing; I've been soft on this. And this was before I read your last brief statement in that leaflet, which really helped to tie it into how people think. That I'm not just beating them up, but I'm trying to provoke them to actually think about something seriously.

So, that's something that occurred to me, and I wanted to hear what you have to say about that.

LaRouche: Well, I can say something which may scare some people. Not by intimidation, but simply by telling the facts of the situation that we have. And this has always been the case of mankind.

See, the problem is,—and I've stated this on a number of occasions, and I will state it more emphatically on this occasion, because we're at a very crucial point,—Obama has brought the issue of war, of thermonuclear war, to occur simultaneously within a matter of *seconds* under his program. And it will be a global war, and it will be a matter of *seconds*; it will be a matter of extermination on a global scale.

Now, what are you going to do? You're afraid of being attacked when the guy you're up against has those kinds of policies, those kinds of commitments? What happens?

See, the point is, mankind is often,—in military affairs, members of the United States have been killed in

creative commons/David

The Tomb of the Unknown Soldier at Arlington National Cemetery outside Washington, D.C.

great numbers in the First World War, the Second World War, and some other conditions which came up more locally. And these people have laid down their lives. Why did they lay down their lives? It was because they had a sense of commitment, of personal commitment, not to be a coward, not to be a traitor, not to be an abstainer from the defense of humanity.

And so therefore, in this kind of situation, you have to take the text as it is. That if you're going to fight this enemy, you're going to go fight against him all the way. You're going to fight against him all the way, and count on the number of survivors, to maintain the cause for which you have fought. This was the kind of thing that happened in World War I and World War II. The idea was, the nation would survive, even if some of the people gave their lives to make that possible. You're in such a situation now. It's a different tune. It's a different note. But it's the same issue. It's the same principle.

And, the best chance is, if you have the guts to force the members of Congress and other officials to exert their guts in dumping Obama, it's the best defense you could possibly ever enjoy.

Q: Good afternoon, Mr. LaRouche. This is S— from New York. Recently, I just went and watched the movie "Drone." And I have a few comments and questions. First, an overview of the movie. It was appalling. They recruit teenagers from a young age to join the drone program from video-game internet cafes. The designer of the drones themselves is very apathetic. He says he hopes his drones are used more to stop war, apparently. The international laws that are broken are immense and many.

They go in with a drone without any authorization; specifically this was about Pakistan. The Pakistani government's been sued twice now by an organization who's trying to get rid of the drones altogether.

I'm sorry, I'm trying to put it all together; the movie was just,—it was too much, really.

The Secret of Progress: The Dead!

Basically, it seems like nobody really cares what America is doing. Everybody's afraid. No one wants to stand up and fight. The people fighting in Pakistan have no support. When they want to go protest, and drive from a smaller country that's in between Pakistan and another country, they're actually met by the Pakistani Army and tanks.

So, what can be done? I mean, how can we stop this? How can we decisively—I know impeaching Obama is one of the answers, but 87 other countries have picked up the drone programs themselves. And in the movie they said that, eventually, seeing foreign drones over our own country will be commonplace.

LaRouche: Yes. The problem is simply one of courage. But it's not a matter of formal courage; it's a matter of understanding what the issues of life for mankind and in nations represent. And, therefore, if you know what the facts are, and you have knowledge of the evidence—and I have a certain amount of knowledge of these matters—you simply say, "We're going to win that war."

Now, that's not just a simple declaration, that we are going to go out there and wave our arms, and so forth, and win this war. We're going to understand exactly what this war means, and what the results would be if we caved in to the enemy. And therefore, if you cannot eliminate the enemy, defeat him, then, you're not going

And let me emphasize one thing that I emphasize repeatedly, which most people tend not to attach themselves to. Mankind's greatest prospect lies in people who have died. It lies there because they were better at science and society than anyone else. And what they did is, their very existence gave mankind the means to bring mankind into a higher level.

to have anything. So therefore you have to mobilize yourselves, in order to motivate a larger population to recognize that what you're doing is right and essential. There's never been much of anything else in known history, the history of warfare, and history of struggle in general. That's been the truth.

Now we have hoped, we have hoped and hoped almost futilely that we could bring about what we call peace. Now peace is not quiet. It's not quietness. Peace is the progress of mankind. And let me emphasize one thing that I emphasize repeatedly, which most people tend not to attach themselves to. Mankind's greatest prospect lies in people who have died. It lies there because they were better at science and society than anyone else. And what they did is, their very existence gave mankind the means to bring mankind into a higher level.

Now, for example, one of the greatest sources of corruption is the belief in being personally practical. People who think that life is based on being practical are cowards, and because they are cowards, they are also idiots. The purpose of mankind has always been, as the case of Kepler, for example, or as the case of Nicholas of Cusa,—models of this case,—that if you stand for that, and you can convey the meaning of that, which is the future of mankind, a future which mankind has not heretofore achieved. And that is the highest goal of human achievement.

Now, people are going to die. Human people, historically, always die; except for a few people who made it so far, a handful of people. Everybody else dies. The question is under what conditions they die, and what conditions do their circles of life represent? Do you represent, in your society, a power of creativity for the future of mankind, which mankind has never achieved before? And it's only when you get to the point that you understand that principle, that you find yourself equipped with the ability to make the argument, and sustain the argument which has to be done.

This is not a sacrifice, because you're going to lose your life anyway. You don't live, you don't have a full life. Anybody who's 100 years of age, or even my

age,—that's not really the issue. The issue is what the future of mankind represents. And the future of mankind, means what can you do, for example, in schools? What can you do in educational systems to make the population that you are supposedly educating, achieve a level of achievement in knowledge and effectiveness which mankind has never experienced before? Isn't that the great achievement?

When we look at the history of mankind, we study the history of mankind, as I've studied the history of mankind at some length in the course of my life, it's the people who create a *new* opportunity, a more advanced opportunity, a corrected opportunity,—and it's those people who mean something.

People who work to get by and pass tests, and get rewards,—they are not very important. The only very important people are those whose actions by themselves are a contribution to the improvement of humanity in general. And that's what we all have to concentrate on. That's the only thing that's really redeeming in terms of the history of mankind. Can you produce an achievement for mankind as a whole which has never been achieved on that level before? And if you have a devotion to that goal, and understand the goal, then you are very powerful. Because the history has shown that it's human achievement of that type, which has been the motive force by which mankind has survived and achieved.

Wait a Minute, Obama!

Q: [follow-up] Thank you. I have one other thing on the matter. I was reading an article, and I found out that the four people in the movie, the four pilots, have had their bank accounts turned off, and they aren't allowed to have their money any more. What do you think can be done about that?

LaRouche: I think what we have to do is the same thing. We have to change the laws to the real laws; back to the real laws of the United States. And that's the only solution. Forget the gimmicks.

Q: Good afternoon, sir, my name is S—. I had been

U.S. Army/Sgt. Zach Mott

Obama's 'leadership' has led to scenes like this house in Iraq, obliterated by a U.S. missile strike, throughout Southwest Asia.

with this organization a number of years ago and had to drop out, and now I'm back. And the funny thing is I was talking to Lynne, and I said "Oh, my goodness, I've resubscribed to the *EIR* alert, and I have to make room." So I'm going through old binders, and naturally I asked, I have all these old *EIR* reports, and would you like to have them as part of your library?

So I'm trying to get to bed every night before midnight, but winding up getting to bed at 5 a.m., because what am I doing? I'm reading these old reports! And it's kind of funny, because only the characters change! It's the same thing! Only it's a little worse now.

I go back to remembering the '50s and '60s, the Cold War, past McCarthyism. We grew up with Russia and America in this Cold War. And we were afraid that anyone,—in an insane moment, someone that might pick up that red phone, to initiate a nuclear holocaust. This was on your mind; you were afraid.

Well, now you have the same thing, only it's worse. And I do have a little African expression: "Together the ants will eat the elephant." [LaRouche laughs.] You liked that one?

I also saw in the '70s there was a big push on for globalization, like this was a good thing. In the last *EIR* I read, earlier this week, it's pointing to how Obama is pushing and pulling the President of France to bring him back into line, so to speak, and insisting, like the

little *bully* in the playground, that we have to put Assad down!

"Wait a minute, just a minute. You are not President of the world, Mr. Obama! Where do you get off, where does any official get off, telling a sovereign nation its business, and how to run its affairs? We'll help, we'll do— hey, we weren't invited into Syria! Get the Hell,—get those 50 people out of Syria! You have no business there; you're breaking international law right there." The lawyers should be on him like flies on a pie!

But we just hear about, read about these atrocities.

I feel like Obama and people like him, if we think about this globalization thing, they're like little Hitler-like bullies running around, trying to say "I'm in charge, it's all my decisions. No, you don't matter, you come on my side (and if you don't I can always kill you)." And just all these things are running through my mind up till like 5 or 6 o'clock in the mornings, and I'm going through all those *EIR*s from 2002, 2004, 2005, and some of those sound just like the *EIR* I got Monday or Tuesday!

So, I don't really have a question. I'm 72 years old, I'm 21 years your junior. I've been on this Earth a while, just like you have—and it's like nothing changes, we just have these little boy bullies running the play yard, forcing everybody to see it their way, and "if you don't agree with me, I'll kill you anyway!"

Well, I'd like you to make comments, because I don't really have a question, I'm just sort of in a befuddled state of mind right now. I feel nothing has changed!

Now, on this issue of getting rid of Obama, of course, I agree with you wholeheartedly. We, on an individual basis, what do we do to effect this? Do we start trying to be a bully and pull the arms of our Congressmen, of our Senators? Do we send letters to them? Do we send emails? What do we do? Do we get on the White House phone, and say, "Look! I'd like to see tomorrow! I'd like to see the sunrise! And do you have a special spaceship you're going to escape to another planet? I'd like to know where you intend on going!" [laughter]

So the point is, on this point, every individual human being, in the final analysis, is totally responsible to themselves for the future of mankind. And when people understand that, as I do, that's the best. You have to have a standard of your own life, which is defined for the benefit for all mankind. And you will not compromise that for anything.

You know, within seven days, a nuclear blast will send a poison wave in the air around the *world*. You going to hold your breath? I don't think that'll work. The Earth is—we're gone. We're gone.

So, please respond, sir, because I'm just...

LaRouche's Worry

LaRouche: OK, OK. I can answer that.

Look, I've been running this organization since its birth; I created this organization. And I've stuck to it because,—even though many of the people who were in my organization at different times and so forth, they were not adequate. So, what do I do? I make myself adequate. And I'm still fighting. I wouldn't give up life, if I could avoid it. You know, I'm stubborn, stubbornly old. And people are looking, "What do you do, you're running around still? Aren't you supposed to be in the graveyard someplace?" Well, I'm not. And I'm still active. I sometimes was more frisky than I have been recently, but when you cross me in the right way, my friskiness becomes fulsome.

And that's how it works. And I don't worry about anybody except me. I'm responsible for me, and what I can contribute to any around me. That's it! And I don't have any other standard. I appreciate people who achieve things. I'm happy when I meet it. I'm happy when they are intelligent, and I'm miserable when they are not. But I try to get over that.

So the point is, on this point, every individual human being, in the final analysis, is totally responsible to themselves for the future of mankind. And when people understand that, as I do, that's the best. You have to have a standard of your own life, which is defined for the benefit for all mankind. And you will not compromise that for *anything*. And otherwise, if you don't do that, you become a failure. And I don't intend to be a failure. They may kill me, but I won't be a failure.

Q: Good afternoon, Mr. LaRouche. R— from Brooklyn. And I'll just start right off. I have noticed that Chancellor Merkel of Germany has held fast to her policy of no nuclear energy after Fukushima, even though her green policy has failed completely. When we get Obama out of office, how do we deal with all the Congress, scientists, and other people screaming, "global warming," et cetera. And when we talk to people, when I've talked to people, the reaction I get is that I'm a conspiracy theorist, and after all, "everybody knows global warming is happening," and this is what I've been getting.

LaRouche: Well, I don't think you have to worry about that at all. The point is we are an organization, and we have a certain ability if we want to conjure up that ability that we have; we can always do something better, a better contribution.

Now you're dealing with the society, what have you got? A bunch of people, a whole bunch of people. Now the question is, can that bunch of people be on the positive side or the negative side, in terms of the next operation?

I have to worry about my responsibilities. And I wish that everybody else would do the same thing: devote themselves to what is an intelligent understanding of what should be their obligations. I try to do that. I hope that other people try to do that. And that's the only chance that mankind has.

Now we've got people who are scientific achievers, real scientific achievers. Now, naturally such people like that, or people of comparable abilities, are much more important for mankind than the other people. But what you have to do, you've got mankind as mankind is given. What you're trying to do is to induce people, all kinds of strata of people, to induce them to bring the best of themselves into contributions for the missions to be held. That's all it is; that's the only answer. I try to be the best I can, and I understand that principle.

I also understand that what we depend upon, is the development of children who are smarter than any other persons ever born. They are the ones who are the creative force, like Einstein, a person of individual characteristics, a superior force of ideas. And that's what you want. You want more Einsteins, and you want more people like that, who can fill in that kind of operation.

And therefore we want to change the school systems

of the United States, and get rid of the kind of school systems that have been dropped on the United States since the beginning of—well, I could name a number of Presidents, a good number of people, but Einstein is an example. Einstein's quality of genius was unique in history of science, *absolutely unique!* And what we need is, we need more Einsteins; that is, the person who can create the ability to foresee the efficient element of the future! Which is what he did. His life was devoted to that intention.

Don't Let Up on Them

And we don't have enough Einsteins. And what we need is, we need a school system which is dedicated to the principle of education for Einstein; to eliminate the garbage, to eliminate the crap, the fakery, to discover the future of mankind. And very few people, even in the history of physical science, have had much capability in that respect.

So the problem is *ours*. We are alive. The problem is ours. The solution is, can we muster in ourselves those qualities of achievement, which will be a serious contribution in the direction of the future of mankind, in the direction of Einstein? The model of Einstein can be a figure used to say, "Here's what we mean by the principle of genius." When the whole rest of the planet was missing on that one. And look at the school systems that have no understanding of Einstein—*none*, absolutely none. Deadheads! Deadheads with a crayon, a piece of chalk on a board, or something. And that's the point.

It is our responsibility to look inside ourselves to recognize those principles to the degree we understand them, and to encourage the people around us to share that view. And then mankind becomes a unit. When mankind can share with other human beings this kind of concern for mankind, then you have a society that works. And right now we have a very poor quality of performance. We have to change that.

And we *can* do it. We can do it right here, right in this place, this premise, tonight, today. We can take steps which will produce a better feature of mankind's behavior than before. And that's the best thing you can count on. You take the person of the poorest quality of development of achievement, or the best, and you just keep pushing it. Don't let them up; don't let them up. Make them go ahead to higher level of achievement.

Don't be practical; practical people are stupid

The genius Albert Einstein

people. We don't want practical people. We may have to use them, but we wish we really didn't have to use them.

Q: [follow-up] I agree with you 100%. Thank you. . . .

Q: Good afternoon, Mr. LaRouche. I have a scientific question. What is antimatter?

LaRouche: Oh! Well, I think that is something which is really obtuse. There is such a description of antimatter, but what is often meant by it, in general, doesn't make much sense. There are some people who have a view of that matter which is relevant, but in general the popular opinion is not relevant. And so, the question of antimatter as a principle,—yes, there what is such a notion of antimatter, but what is generally represented as the subject of antimatter is simply doubletalk.

Q: I just want to get your spin on this: You don't have Einsteins because people have been trained to think in mathematics, and not in concepts. Whereas Einstein, his ideas are his concepts. $E=mc^2$, energy is equal to speed of light squared and mass, which is a concept. Time is not a definite thing, it depends upon the observer. What is your spin on that?

LaRouche: Well, I think the question of Einstein's work is—just take his principal works. He had certain benchmarks in terms of the stages of his development. And it led up to the end of his life. So, Einstein is a unique figure, and almost, except for some very exceptional cases, Einstein is the only complete scientist that I would consider a true scientist.

The problem was, is, that with the beginning of Bertrand Russell's entry into the name of science, since that time, science in the Twentieth Century went through a process of practiced degeneration. That's what has to be said about it all. These were all practical people, they were mathematicians, and the worst thing you can get in science is a devoted mathematician. It's the worst thing that can be done to you.

And therefore, if you don't have what Einstein understood,—which is his approach by steps to make an ever deeper insight into what man's role is in the universe,—and that's what his theme is all the way through. What is man's role in the universe? If you want to take all the Einstein works that I know of, it all boils down to that issue.

What the differences were between Einstein and his opponents, were exactly of that nature. And what we need to do is we need to really emphasize Einstein, and start over again, with people who are a little bit better educated than the majority we've had so far.

But Einstein's method, his approach to life, is absolutely unique. And other scientists, some of them had approaches to him; some people borrowed from him aspects of what he's done. But no man that I know of has had a fulsome realization of the quality of action which Einstein and his living characteristics had represented. He's just the genius, the leading genius on the records of books.

Cooperate with Each Other

Q: Good afternoon, Mr. LaRouche, this is I__M__, how are you today? I've been reading the *EIR* and I must say, they have been really informative, and I just want to thank you for your job that you have been doing for a very long time, and I think there should have been more people like you. Because—

LaRouche: My enemies don't agree with that!

Q: [follow-up] You look out for humanity, which is very good. But I have to think about my region, the Caribbean, and we have been shafted by the isms and schisms of all the different nationalities. But I think, coming here and being here most every Saturday has been good for me, because I'm able to talk to other people who are Caribbean and let them know there is someone who is not a fear-minded person, and I hope one day I will get them to come to a meeting.

But getting back to the Syrian situation now, I think it was a situation just waiting to happen. Because there are so many people involved, and most people don't know about the core of the problem, so I think what you have been saying all the time surely made sense, and I'm looking forward to a response from you, as to what you think can deviate World War III.

LaRouche: Well, I think one thing, you're talking about Central and South America, that area in particular: One of my first heroes, was José López Portillo of Mexico. And he was the head of Mexico at that point, and I collaborated with him, and we had a meeting in his office, and we loosed things out! We really went at it! And we did an excellent job: We changed the whole Mexico system, improved it; he was a genius. And then he was crushed. Mexico was crushed.

And in terms of South America and in the Caribbean area, I've seen similar cases, with some exceptions, with similar nations which have been crushed: Colombia has been crushed; other parts of South America have been crushed again, repeatedly. And we have a few that sort of got by with it once in a while. But most of South and Central America have been crushed.

Now, part of the problem comes from Wall Street and the British,—that's generally the problem. Wall Street and the British are the enemies of Central and South America; if there's anything wrong with Central and South America in general, it's to be blamed on the British and Wall Street. Get rid of those two sins, you might have a better chance.

Q: [follow-up] OK. Most of the English-speaking islands were once former British colonies, and they occupy the Lesser Antilles. But you know, despite the British, other people tried to intimidate and use racism against the Black people there.

LaRouche: Ah. This is stuff which disgusts me. Let's forget it, let's get rid of it! We've got—

Q: [follow-up] You can't! But you can't, because so many people are not conscious. The level of consciousness there, they're selling out.

LaRouche: All we have to do, is we have to cooperate with each other. That's all. That's the only chance we have. It's what we can do to cooperate with each other and to get an influence on the process of society which will enable us to be free from some of the things that have been disgusting.

JFK Library/Abbie Rowe

The promise of cooperation: President John Kennedy with Peruvian President Manuel Prado at the White House in September 1961.

Q: Good afternoon, Mr. LaRouche. Thank you for taking my question. My name is M__ B__. I'm a local in New York. So, I've seen on the news lately and it's very disturbing about this organization in Turkey, the Grey Wolves. And this is a Gladio B operation that's been set up. And they're ready to move, and do things; they had a truckload recently in Italy was intercepted with a bunch of shotguns in it; and they have bike gangs in Germany. They're all around. It seems to be something of concern. Do you know anything about it?

Not That Simple

LaRouche: I know some things about some parts of these kinds of things in general; naturally, at my age and experience, there are a lot of things I know! But there are also, in the process of bypassing, a lot of things that I've skipped or have not been brought in on, on other things. I'm not a universal person as applied to all subjects, but I do have a pretty good idea of what's going on in the world. I think that's what you can say.

And you know, the world is now—what I'm worried about all the time, what I've been concerned about, is the things I think I can do something about. And I pick out those things which I find that I have the strongest objections to; and what I think I can do something about. And so I concentrate on that.

And the problem is there's a shortage of people, who—but sometimes, they come across for you. Sometimes. You know, people in Germany, for example, sometimes are a disappointment to me; people in France who are a disappointment, a recent case. The French case.

Now France has been a disgusting nation for a long period of time. But suddenly, when it got into this crisis, of terror rage, and when they got into connection with the issue of the relationship between France and the Mediterranean region, France came out and did something good. Something better than they've done for a long period of time; and I appreciate that. I'm not satisfied with it, but it's much better than what I've seen before.

And so my views on these kinds of things take those colors. There are a lot of things I have no access to, or almost no access to. Some things that I've had great access to, in certain periods, like my experience with Russia for a long period of time; and that was nice. But I have limitations, and I have to operate on the basis of limitations of a broad background of experience.

Q: My name is J__. My question is, why everybody is so scared to try to impeach Obama, is because, I believe, we're scared to do that because of his complexion. If we try to get him out, everybody's going to think why we're doing that because of what color he is. Not because of what's going on. So that's what this country has become, that we're too scared to really say what's wrong with him, and go after him for the crimes he's committing. But we won't do that, because others might think, society might think we're going after him because he's African American. And that's what I think.

LaRouche: Well, things are not that simple. I have a responsibility and I have probably much more knowledge, because of my age, than a lot of people in various parts of the world. But I have limitations too. And therefore, I don't think we can make simplistic characterizations of what the situation is.

I think what we have to do is try to find the aperture

in which we can create an influence to build something positive within society. A lot of things don't lend themselves to becoming characteristic; but whatever we can do that's good, do it! And in terms of generalities,—I don't really have much confidence in generalities,—but I do have the intention to improve: Yes, that I like.

Speed: By way of partially responding, Lyn, myself, to what was just raised, this is a report we got from Sean Stone. He wanted this raised to you, because everybody's on their way to Paris now for the climate change conference. There's going to be 191 heads of state.

So he wanted to make sure you are aware of this: There was a contro-

White House video

President Obama addreses the 'Conference of Depopulation' in Paris on Nov. 30.

versy this past February because a movie was released in England which portrayed—it was only a portion of the movie, but it portrayed Barack Obama as a member of a plot to kill 99% of the world population. And so, it was sort of a comic thing: What it is, there's a megalomaniac who sits down, and he's shown speaking to Obama about global warming, and the megalomaniac is saying, "Look, I've checked. There's no way, the science all comes out, as long as you have people on the planet, you're going to have global warming, so all we can do is,—I've got an idea and it's to wipe everybody out."

So the President agrees, OK? Everybody's got to be eliminated: he becomes part of the plot. So then, the director and writer of the film have insisted it isn't Obama, but the problem is, you can tell by the ears, that back of the head, and the vision of the White House in the background! It's definitely Obama.

Obama Must be Removed!

So what happens is: he can't be trusted, though, so they put an implant in his head, to make sure he can be kept under control. So then, Sean sent me—this is an excerpt from an actual review of this movie; it says, I'm quoting now:

> Barack Obama's head explodes, because he's in on the supervillain's dastardly plot. Seriously,

this is the thing that happens in this movie, and it's sort of surprising that nobody's made a big deal out of it. Because it's pretty rare for movies to kill off a sitting President by suggesting he's in on an evil plot. Granted the President is never named, but he's got the recognizable profile, and the brief impression of him is clearly meant to sound Obama-esque. And the sequence where his head and the heads of his Joint Chiefs of Staff, explode, is cartoonishly fun. But it's still weird to have the President,—like a clear signifier of the actual President,—involved in a plot to kill something like 99% of the world's population.

And then it goes on to say, "No other people, all others are fictionalized; the only other one that you can identify, is the Queen of England." [laughter]

So I thought I'd put that in as a form of an intelligence report and a bit of a response to the question that you just got.

LaRouche: OK! I think it's quite relevant. Have fun with it! It's all your own.

Q: Hi, Lyn. I'm relaying a question from R__ from Bergen County, who's tied up tutoring today. His question is the following: "I have a sense that Obama is becoming increasingly hated within the population. That the perception is that ISIS is being supported by Obama because he is doing nothing. My question is, what position will Congress be in, if ISIS attacks the United States, with Congress increasingly aligned with Obama, by its failure to act on this?"

LaRouche: Well, I think it's a moot point. Because there's another approach that you have to take on this thing. Obama and what he represents has to be shut down. In other words, there are no intervening steps. Shut this guy down, because the defense of the human species depends upon accomplishing that effect. That's exactly what has to happen.

Look at the history of Obama: Obama's stepfather was famous for mass murder: He was a colonel in an operation of mass murder in southern waters. And Obama himself was trained by the stepfather. He has the same characteristics, known to us, as the stepfather,—and the mother of Obama was also of the same quality: So what do you expect with such working material?

Therefore, Obama must be removed from all control, political control of all governments on the planet, *all* governments of the planet. He is a disease which must be closed off on now. We must never see anything like Obama appearing in political life ever again. Because you can't trust him. He's intrinsically Satanic. The only name you can give, in history, is that his quality is entirely Satanic, literally Satanic. And you don't want to cook him, because it's also poisonous.

Speed: OK, I guess we're now at our conclusion, Lyn. So, I don't know if there's anything else—Oh! I'd like to ask you this. So of course, we're going to go into a new phase now in Manhattan, because of the focus that we've now been given from you, on the Obama matter. We'll be doing a lot of things on the music, and matter of fact, we have a major rehearsal tonight that Diane is going to be running, and John is here as well. So we're about to go into that.

And I don't know if there's anything that you have specific that you'd like to say, or are we...?

LaRouche: No, it's an ongoing process. And let the process unfold as it wishes to.

Speed: All right. Very good. So that's it for us today. So I'd like everybody to join me to say to you once again: Thanks a lot! [applause]

LaRouche: Have fun!

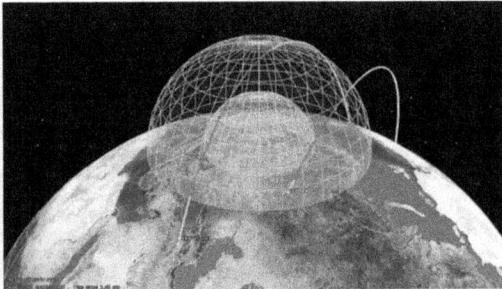

You Have Very Little Time To Change Your Thinking

Dec. 2—Bob Wesser interviews Phil Rubinstein on Roosevelt's struggle with polio.

In an Emergency Nationwide Fireside Chat on Nov. 25, Thanksgiving eve, when the world stood on the brink of war after Turkey had downed a Russian bomber, Lyndon LaRouche said that the American people have to mobilize to educate themselves, and to grasp that the values that they have been taught to adopt, have actually corrupted them. It's not just a question of cleaning up people in general, but that people have to be brought to understand that there are certain diseases with which they themselves have infected their own minds. But how can you ask them to do that if you haven't done it yourself? You can't.

Wesser: Recently Mr. LaRouche, in a discussion with associates, addressed the question of the required leadership today. And in this regard, the example of the shift in thinking of Franklin D. Roosevelt was brought up, and I understand you have a few comments on that.

Rubinstein: Yes, I think that FDR is a very interesting case, because the matter must be seen from the standpoint of leadership; because he was part of a patrician class, if you want to call it that, in the United States, and he was a political person from the time he was in his late twenties. He was elected to office; he was a State Representative and so forth. And he thought of himself as being a leader with a potential leadership in the future.

But he had a certain level of illusion,—and in fact, in the early part of the Twentieth Century, the country was going through some of the worst leadership possible in Teddy Roosevelt and Woodrow Wilson, both of whom were Confederate sympathizers, or even Con-

FDR Presidential Library & Museum

Franklin D. Roosevelt and his wife Eleanor aboard a campaign train during his 1932 run for the Presidency.

federates themselves,—and the country was headed into a great crisis. FDR was political, was against corruption, and was not a bad person, but I think he was limited. He owed a great deal to his reasonable appearance, his background, a quality of intelligence,—and some ambition. He had the ambition to be a political leader. But he certainly was not prepared for the crises that the country was about to face. Not only going through World War I, but of course, the collapse of the economy into the Great Depression, much of which was already underway in the mid-1920s in the farm sector, which he was aware of.

Now, what was it that made Roosevelt the leader that he became, which came to fruition in his Governorship in 1928,—what made him capable of taking on Wall Street in 1932 and 1933? As he uniquely did, and said so specifically, which is something like the kind of courage that we need from ourselves and from political leaders today, with respect to Obama and Wall Street. They have to be removed! We have to have people with the courage to say, "We don't need these people, we don't need this leadership, this is evil."

What gave Franklin Roosevelt, a relatively, shall we

say, somewhat superficial political figure when he was first elected to political office, and when he was Assistant Secretary of the Navy during World War I,—he may have done some good things, but he was far short of being the unique leader that led the world through the Depression and the War, and to this day remains the legacy, the point of reference,—not of imitation simply, in the sense of formal imitation,—but in the sense of imitating his courage. And I think what we know about this situation is the crisis that he went through on contracting polio at the age of 39, where he had just run for Vice President; he was an up-and-coming politician, etc., and now, his entire life was undermined.

FDR Presidential Library & Museum

Three years after being stricken by polio, FDR begins to re-enter politics. Here he greets New York politicians, including Gov. Al Smith (to FDR's right), in August of 1924.

Why? Partly because of appearances. The appearance of weakness, the inability to walk,—and of course, this was deeply depressing. We know that Franklin Roosevelt went through deep depression. Like many people, he tried to convince himself he was going to walk again. He struggled to make himself somewhat mobile. There are some things that almost make you wince even hearing them. Once I went out to Hyde Park, and he described dragging himself down the road to the entrance of Hyde Park,—I think it was a mile or more,—and he literally dragged himself down that road to build strength, thinking that eventually he could walk. Much of this is well known now,—the heavy metal braces he had to wear later on. In fact, this is part of why the British knew that eventually he would die at a relatively young age,—because of the consequences of being a paraplegic.

But what he did during that period, was he recognized that his physical presence was not the essential nature of his being. He was a human being. He had a mind. Other human beings had minds. And so, he went through, not just a reflection on himself, but he began to recognize what he had to be, to be a real leader to lift people out of weakness.

An Optimistic View

His Labor Secretary, Frances Perkins, was one of the few people who worked with him through the Gov-

ernorship, the whole period, knew him during this entire period. She had been herself very significant in New York, and she said, later on, that he didn't really like people very much (this is as a younger man). She said he had

a youthful lack of humility, a streak of self-righteousness, and a deafness to the hopes, fears and aspirations which are the common lot. The marvel is that these handicaps were washed out of him by life, experience, punishment, and his capacity to grow. He once said to me when he was President, "You know, I was an awfully mean cuss, when I first went into politics."

She goes on to say that Franklin Roosevelt underwent a spiritual transformation during the years of his illness.

I noticed that he came back, that the years of pain and suffering had purged the slightly arrogant attitude. The man emerged completely warm-hearted, with humility of spirit and with a deeper philosophy. Having been to the depths of trouble, he understood the problems of people in trouble. He believed that Divine Providence had intervened to save him from total paralysis, despair and death.

So, that is one reflection.

Eleanor Roosevelt talks about the way in which he became a deeper person. He had a more open sense of other human beings. And I think there was an intellectual development. Things that he may have believed somewhat, an orientation through some of his family ties to Alexander Hamilton,—this became deeper. He studied the history of the United States, the founding of the United States. He even began a book, which I do not think he got that far on, but he did a lot of work on it. He began to understand what the founding of the United States was about. So, when he was the President and earlier Governor, he, like Hamilton, took on the financiers,—and, in fact, even more, Roosevelt took on Wall Street, which had destroyed the United States.

So it was both. These are not separate: it was an emotional development, it was a reflection on himself, and an intellectual development, bringing together the courage to fight for certain ideas. And that really was the unique development of a leader in the Twentieth Century who saved the United States, who saved the world from Fascism and its consequences. This is the kind of depth that is required to effectively challenge the presumptive leadership today, which has failed to remove Obama, and failed to shut down Wall Street,— and there are other examples of this in history, which I think are similar.

Wesser: To follow up on this. This is quite fascinating, because the whole discussion came up in Mr. La-Rouche's emergency Fireside Chat of last Wednesday, in response to a gentleman enquiring, "How are we going to get the American people to rise up and demand Obama's ouster?" And LaRouche said, "Well there is no systemic principle inherent in anybody that is preventing this." So this is quite an optimistic view, and I guess what you are getting at here is that this is something that is universal.

Rubinstein: Right, and in fact, I will give you a very interesting other example, which is the case of Beethoven. Whereas, people know, he lost his hearing,—actually he lost his hearing in the late 1790s, when he was probably in his mid-20s. He wrote a famous statement called the *Heiligenstadt Testament*, which he kept for himself,—he wrote it to his brothers,

but I don't think he ever actually sent it to his brothers, and he writes this in 1802, when he is in his early thirties. But he says his hearing had been deteriorating for seven years, and then he says that it was "only my art which held me back," and he means from ending his life. "So it seemed it was impossible to me to leave this world before I produced all that I felt capable of producing. So I prolonged this wretched existence."

Now, what did he do in prolonging his existence? I mean, he was already a virtuoso, but now he was dedicated to developing musical art to the level of inspiring populations to making the necessary political changes,— to bring forth the development of other human beings like himself, for he was, as they would say in those days, a commoner. And, of course, he did, and much of his great work was produced, in his case, later in his life, after this. For him it was art, he lived for art.

He Could Bring them Back

I think in the case of Franklin Roosevelt, he knew he was a political leader, a practitioner of what Friedrich Schiller called the "highest form of art," statecraft. That was Franklin Roosevelt's calling. Initially, somewhat from the standpoint of the *noblesse oblige* of a patrician. That was when he was a younger man. Now what he goes through—he couldn't walk—now he lost all the things that were part of his personal appearance. He was six feet two inches tall, good-looking, bright, and so on and so forth, charming. I don't think he was too superficial, but he was limited. What he saw with the polio, was that all those things are ephemeral. What you really are, is not just your mind, but your willingness to take on a mission of producing something for humanity's future.

I think it is interesting, for example, that he was preoccupied in a different way with Warm Springs. He would go there all the time, and he loved to spend time with the people who came there. He created Warm Springs as kind of a cure place for polio victims, and he would spend the time with them. He called for research into polio, but he wanted to spend time with these people. He made the point that everybody who came to Warm Springs showed signs of improvement.

I think that was something of a way-station in his development, which he always recognized the importance of for him, for himself, for his own development. He was giving to other people, and he saw the need to do that, and he saw what you could get. You could bring people back from despair; you could bring them back from depression, you could even bring them back from medical illness. And he saw this as a social obligation, so when he became the Governor of New York,—as I said, he always maintained his attachment to Warm Springs,—but when he became the Governor of New York, he was the one who implemented what would become the predecessors of unemployment insurance, of the federal guarantee for banking deposits, ultimately Social Security, and other such related phenomena.

As I said, he took on Wall Street; he basically took over public infrastructure. Now Warm Springs was an exemplification of much of that. It was a very different person, who had a very different sense of identity, but it was a political sense of identity. And this was his mission in life, to which he was dedicated,—and he learned something about what the nature of that mission was; and he dedicated himself to that future.

Eleanor Roosevelt, during his period of— really going through this crisis— she went out and basically represented their political view for the first time in her life, and though I don't think she would have called it that, she was a political spokesperson. She also of course, worked with him,—though it was a very difficult time,—through the poliomyelitis, and this whole experience of Warm Springs. He created the spa,—he created this,—and then he came back and there were ten patients, then seventeen patients, and he went before the Medical Board and said that these people were showing improvement. I mean, he probably hoped for a cure. But this was a powerful statement about a disease that only produced despair.

And what Lyn [LaRouche] was saying Wednesday night, is people say "How do you do it?"—"You can't do it," "We're impotent," and they wallow in a certain kind of despair. Well, Franklin Roosevelt faced a certain depth of despair, and answered by, in a sense, elevating himself; teaching himself history, teaching himself elements of economics. And becoming thereby not only a better person, but developing in himself a sense of mission, that gave him the kind of courage to do what no other political leader dared to do. The failure of that quality of leadership is what happened in Germany.

Wesser: So I guess you would say that, in the case of Franklin Roosevelt, not only was he very, very close to death itself,—he barely survived the disease,—but

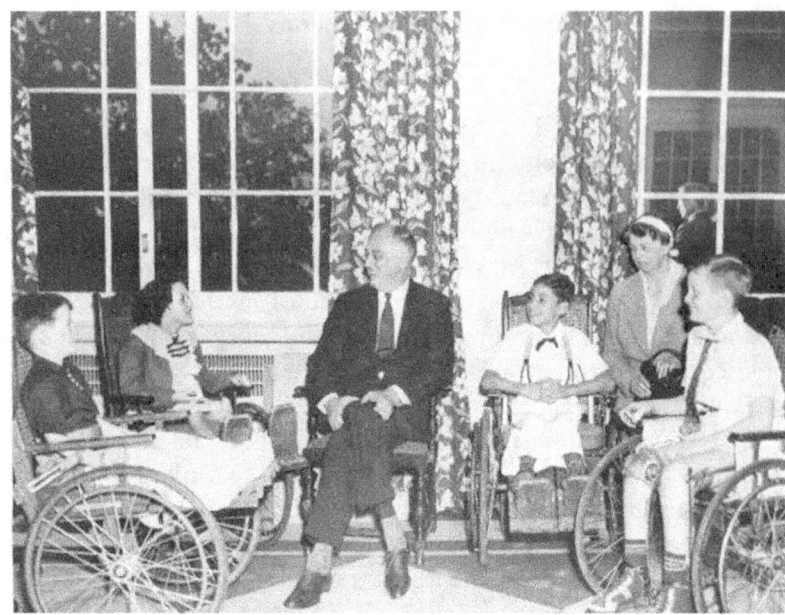

FDR talks with fellow polio patients in Warm Springs, Georgia, the rehabilitation facility which he funded, and was open to any polio victim in the country.

he then understood also, I believe, that his life was not going to be long. This was not a man who would have longevity, and in a certain sense, then, committed himself, in the way you are posing it, to defeating death, or achieving a certain kind of immortality,—but in a political field,—which at that point was vital to the United States and the entire world.

Rubinstein: Yes, he committed himself to the future of humanity. Later in his life, of course, he ran for a fourth term, I think there is some truth in what you are saying. People did not live long; medical circumstances were quite different; polio itself was often fatal. He was aware, at least, of that. To the very end of his life, he put himself on the line. At Yalta, for example, he was often criticized, but he knew exactly what he was doing at Yalta. And, for example, he knew that he had to negotiate with Stalin; he knew what the Russians had gone through in World War II. He stood as a bulwark against Churchill and Churchill's desire to go to war,—and the fact that he had, at the age of 62, suffered twenty years or more as a paraplegic, did not stop him.

And, of course, had he lived, he had a vision of what the United Nations should be, and so forth, and he had the partnership of Eleanor during all this, despite the slanders against them. And in that sense his mission in life is what guided his leadership beyond all other concerns, including concerns for his simple mortal life.

What is the Manhattan Project?

by Dennis Speed

On condition that we show, that classical fine art depends upon the generating function of the same individual creative mental processes otherwise responsible for the generation and assimilation of valid fundamental scientific discoveries, and only on condition of that proof, are we able to supply valid general statements about "human nature."

—Lyndon H. LaRouche,
"Beethoven as a Physical Scientist,"
May 1989

It was not 'til the last session that I became unequivocally convinced of the following truth—That Mr. Madison cooperating with Mr. Jefferson is at the head of a faction decidedly hostile to me and my administration, and actuated by views in my judgement subversive of the principles of good government and dangerous to the union, peace and happiness of this country.

—Alexander Hamilton,
letter to Edward Carrington,
May 26, 1792

Nov. 29—The LaRouche "Manhattan Project" is the resurrection of Alexander Hamilton's United States in New York City. That United States cannot coexist with Wall Street.

Every Saturday afternoon, since late June 2015, Lyndon LaRouche engages in a face-to-face, and "mind to mind," dialogue with a self-selected sample from the population of New York City. Schoolteachers, baggage handlers, musicians, retired professionals, and students participate. This dialogue, and what flows from it, is called "the Manhattan Project." As with its World War Two predecessor, born of the desperate necessity to achieve a scientific breakthrough, this contemporary Manhattan Project is a "crash program," but with a difference. Instead of "success" being defined by the timely discovery of a new means of deployment of physical principles, resulting in the creation of the greatest weapons of mass destruction ever devised, the LaRouche Manhattan Project is designed to unleash the dormant power of the American citizenry to take back its government.

In current history's present moments, unfortunately defined by the bone-headed Obama Administration—a "strange beast, slouching toward Armageddon"—and its sullen, sneering provocation of general thermonuclear war, the Saturday LaRouche dialogue is an essential process, and an exceptional one. The sense of solidarity among the citizenry that once emboldened the United States to "take arms against a sea of troubles, and, by opposing, end them," has all but been eradicated. This, however, can be revivified, and even instantaneously so, as has been demonstrated by the varied exchanges among participants in the discussions with LaRouche these past five months.

The Process

A short opening statement is given by LaRouche, or sometimes not. Each person then steps to the microphone and states a question, concern, or report. Then "the fun begins." The back and forth is not "pair-wise," as it might appear. Rather, representative government, in the person or the "assembled body" of the chorus-audience, deliberates. The struggle to formulate what the

clipart.com

Alexander Hamilton as a young caption of the Artillery in New York City in 1776. Here, he salutes General Washington.

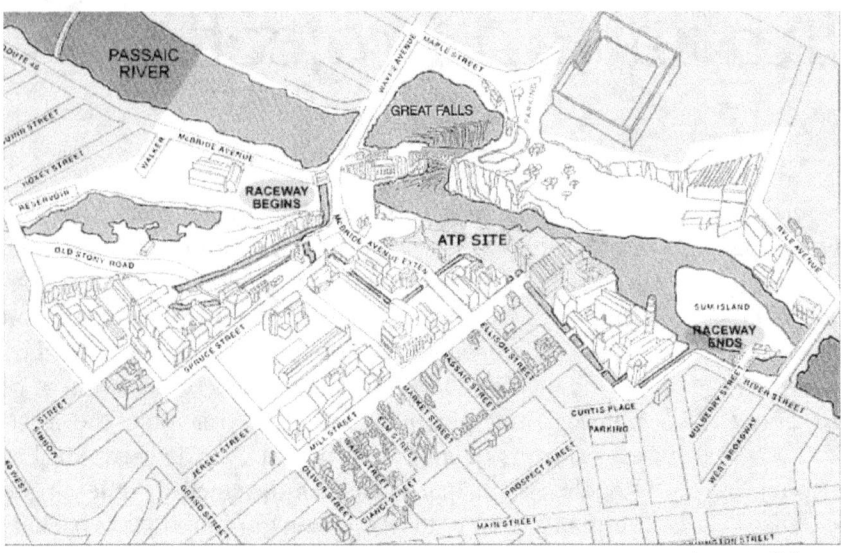

patersongreatfalls.com

Hamilton's Vision: A schematic of Hamilton's plan for the Society for Establishing Useful Manufactures, built on the Passaic Falls (Great Falls), New Jersey. The design for the advanced waterworks and manufacturing complex was done by Pierre L'Enfant. The ATP site stands for Allied Textile Printing, and is the location of the SEUM's original textile mills, which were in operation for 200 years.

real questions of policy must be for our nation, and to better our nation by removing from the Presidency the "democratic tyranny" of the last fourteen years' Bush/Cheney-Obama Administration, is a pedagogical exercise led by LaRouche, at the conclusion of which, people leave the assembly better than when they arrived.

It was this deliberative and self-governing process that Alexander Hamilton had always intended for the free, singular, and sovereign republic of the United States. Alexander Hamilton's two Presidential co-terms with George Washington, extending from April 30, 1789 until eight years later in 1797, however, espoused principles that were completely rejected by those "Confederacy-minded" co-founders of the nation such as Thomas Jefferson, whose Third Presidency began on March 4, 1801.

LaRouche in October of 2014 initiated the Manhattan Project expressly to resurrect the principle of Alexander Hamilton's New York and United States—to create and empower the most productive, literate, and skilled free citizenry in the world, exerting and improving the productive powers of its labor, impeded not by ethnic background, skin color or lack of title, but only by the limitations of human creativity—which has *no* limitations.

Nothing *but* limitations on the United States, how-

ever, will exist so long as Wall Street, which sits geographically and morally at the bottom of Manhattan, is allowed to continue to exist. Hamilton was assassinated by the original "child of Satan," Aaron Burr, and his Bank of Manhattan, directly and consciously on behalf of the militarily defeated British Empire. Various contemporary ongoing attempts to re-assassinate Hamilton, including the current weird Broadway hip-hop musical "about his life," and the drive to remove his visage from the ten-dollar bill, underscore Wall Street's ongoing treasonous role, and the present President Obama's spiritual descent—if that is possible—from British agents Aaron Burr, Martin Van Buren, Fernando Wood, August Belmont, Robert Moses, and Felix Rohatyn.

Washington, Hamilton, and Hamilton's mentor Benjamin Franklin, as well as Hamilton's close friends, New Yorkers Gouverneur Morris and John Jay, after successfully crafting between 1787 and 1789 what would come to be adopted as the United States Constitution, established the economic foundation for an independent sovereign nation for the first time in world history. The Society for Establishing Useful Manufactures (SEUM) set up by Hamilton and collaborators in Paterson, New Jersey; the great Erie Canal project (in the which Phillip Schuyler, Hamilton's father-in-law, had played a major role); the development of the West Point Military Academy and the American engineering corps (Treasury Secretary Hamilton purchased the land for it in 1790); and the expansion and fortification of the Port of New York, were expressions of the real intent behind the Preamble of the United States Constitution.

Hamilton, Jay, and Morris' fierce, though unsuccessful, battle against slavery at the 1787 Constitutional Convention, merely convinced Hamilton *and Washington* all the more, that manufacturing, industry, and internal improvements such as the Potomac and Erie Canal systems (later, under Lincoln, transcontinental rail systems) were the means for the permanent liberation of the new nation from its recently-broken thralldom to the still-dominant British Empire. (Alexander Hamilton and John Jay, Hamilton's collaborator in writing the *Federalist* papers, co-founded the New

Wall Street's agent Aaron Burr depicted assassinating Hamilton in Weehawken, N.J. on July 11, 1804.

York Manumission Society in 1785. Slavery was partially abolished in New York State in 1799, and was then fully abolished in 1827.) Revolutionary technological breakthroughs, and the "taming of nature and fate" through new forms of power, like the application of steam-engine power, were the hallmark of the American character, what was sometimes referred to as "American Know-How," or "Can-Do."

LaRouche On Manhattan: Winning the War

In November 2014, LaRouche revealed the principle of Alexander Hamilton's Manhattan to his associates: "... my first impression of this sort of thing: I was in New York City. It was at the time of the launching of the [Second World] war against the United States. And I was walking on a tour, on Sunday, to go to a business meeting.... And then I heard the voice of President Roosevelt speaking, and soon enough I got the message. And most of the citizens of New York City in particular were rushing to places to sign up for warfare, who didn't even know what warfare was, or didn't know where to go to register... And that is exactly what the New York spirit represents. That's what it embodies, when it functions."

He continued: "You have to centralize our organization as a *national organization*. And the best way to do that, is with Manhattan. If you establish the principle of Manhattan as being a rallying point for the nation as a whole, a rallying point based on a principle, based on a passion, into which people are captured, *then* you can beat the enemy! It doesn't guarantee you're going to, but you can, then. If you do what you've been doing heretofore, you will never beat the enemy."

(A year later, he reported this evaluation to the now-weekly Manhattan audience: "Okay, well, we're at an opportune moment, where we're ready to produce our own ability to project the kind of conception of organization which is required at this time. This is the moment of readiness where we can move to take over in the process of our party, our own political organization.")

The Manhattan Project has incorporated the best elements of the "deployment repertoire" of LaRouche forces over decades. Rallies on Wall Street don't just discuss "the economy" or "re-instating the Glass-Steagall Act." Classical music is performed there by members of the recently-established Schiller Institute New York Community Choir, both satirical and straightforward. Sometimes the Queen of England, or Barack Obama, or their sponsor, Satan, also join the rallies. Leaflets are distributed and literature is given out; the international audience that characterizes Wall Street learns that there is an American faction that is co-organizing, with a comprehensive unique-in-the-world report, the new world scientific and economic revolution that is presently headquartered in the BRICS nations, particularly China.

When the United Nations opened in September, Manhattan Project organizers were there, opposing the UN's "global warming/climate change" depopulation policy. Even more important, LaRouche *anticipated* and prepared New Yorkers for the strategic "ass-whipping" that Vladimir Putin delivered to a befuddled Obama in Syria, revealing the latter's *de facto* support for the very ISIS grouping that he claimed to oppose.

Interventions challenging the policy outlook of the "financial elite" have personally challenged former Fed chief Ben Bernanke, Obama's Timothy Geithner, and Mervyn King, the former head of the Bank of England on their own turf, be that a university, a bookstore, or church. Table deployments in downtowns, in the subways, and at local sites like post offices or stores, allow for the organizers to obtain a first-hand evaluation of what people *really* think. This is generally otherwise completely unknown, or made unavailable, kept that

Hamilton revived: A poster being deployed by LaRouche's Manhattan Project shows Alexander Hamilton as the sixth member of the BRICS leadership.

way especially through the fraud known as "public opinion polling."

Weekly phone calls, including a Thursday call also featuring LaRouche, allow citizens to incorporate important developments and changes in the world strategic situation into their thinking, allowing for a rapid re-conceptualization of the national focus and intention of the week. Now the citizen is supplied the conceptual basis, through a daily briefing and weekly discussion from which thinking must start.

No 'Information, Please'!!!

The Manhattan Project is the most "impractical" political process that could be devised. Some organizers are fond of pointing out that "if you think you know what the Manhattan project is, then you have probably lost touch with the whole process." Perhaps the best way to convey what is meant here, is to refer to the remarks LaRouche made in an answer to a question this last Saturday, November 27.

Referring to himself, he said, "many of the people who were in my organization at different times and so forth, they were not adequate. So what do I do? I make *myself* adequate. And I'm still fighting... And I don't worry about anybody except me. I'm responsible for me, and what I contribute to any around me. That's it! And I don't have any other standard.... *So the point is, in this point, every individual human being, in the final analysis, is totally responsible to themselves for the*

future of mankind. And when people understand that, as I do, that's the best."

How does one go about discovering this principle, and conveying it to others? It is not done by "giving information," but by the opposite—by removing disinformation, challenging assumptions, uprooting axioms.

"O Freunde, nicht diese Töne!" "O friends, not these tones," as Beethoven admonishes in the first spoken words of his Ninth Symphony, is, in this sense, the "stretto" of the Saturday LaRouche dialogue. A music class, focused on the Italian *bel canto* method of singing, as well as on *solfège*, given by LaRouche Policy Committee member Diane Sare, usually precedes the policy discussion, because it is an effective way of jamming the noise in the heads of those forced to submit to the mental prison of today's popular sub-culture, and because, as Beethoven's friend Friedrich Schiller pointed out, it is "through Beauty" that one proceeds to "Freedom" of thought. *"Nicht diese Töne"* is the first law of mental hygiene that the Manhattan Project suggests to and requires of all of those who would call themselves responsible and accountable for their nation, and for the world as a whole.

Whether the United States might survive its present head-long, and accelerating, descent into barbarism, cruelty, and chaos, depends upon the citizenry resolving to take back its government from the likes of Barack Obama and the predecessor Cheney/Bush Administration. This cannot be done without starting from the re-assertion of the singular national character of our nation as a sovereign, economically independent, and scientifically progressive republic—not a collection of folksy fiefdoms jokingly referred to as "states," "a confederacy of dunces."

"Nicht diese Töne," but a return to the certain trumpet of Alexander Hamilton's original United States, "that a bolder note than this might swell" from the united voices of America's forgotten citizens, is the purpose, and obligation of the "great experiment" called the Manhattan Project.